QUALITY CONTROL IN HIGHER EDUCATION

Charles P. Hogarth

UNIVERSITY
PRESS OF
AMERICA

LANHAM • NEW YORK • LONDON

Copyright © 1987 by

University Press of America,® Inc.

4720 Boston Way
Lanham, MD 20706

3 Henrietta Street
London WC2E 8LU England

Printed in the United States of America

British Cataloging in Publication Information Available

Library of Congress Cataloging-in-Publication Data

Hogarth, Charles P. (Charles Pinckney), 1911-
Quality control in higher education.

Bibliography: p.
1. Universities and colleges—United States—
Administration. 2. Education, Higher—United States—
Evaluation. 3. Education, Higher—United States—Aims
and objectives. I. Title.
LB2341.H58   1987   378.73   87-2055
ISBN 0-8191-6174-8 (alk. paper)
ISBN 0-8191-6175-6 (pbk. : alk. paper)

All University Press of America books are produced on acid-free
paper which exceeds the minimum standards set by the National
Historical Publication and Records Commission.

DEDICATION

To my wife Nancy, our daughter Nancy Eva,
and our son Charles Jr.

INTRODUCTION

This volume relates the essentials of what is being done in the public and private colleges and universities in the USA, what kind of quality controls enter into the work, and what more should be done to improve the quality of the product. The first chapter outlines many of the off-campus controls, and the other chapters are devoted to the inside operations of higher education.

The discussion has to do with all 3,297 colleges and universities in the USA with 12,247,000 students enrolled. Approximately three-fourths of these students are enrolled in the public colleges and universities. The institutions included are 62 private and 94 public universities, 1388 private and 472 public other four-year institutions, and 356 private and 925 public two-year or community colleges. (Source: Most recent reports from the National Center for Education Statistics and the USA Department of Education).

This volume was written primarily for the general public, governmental groups, prospective college students, students and employees of colleges and universities, and for some people in other countries.

The Appendix includes a few selected references for each chapter in this volume.

TABLE OF CONTENTS

Chapter 1

OUTSIDE CONTROLS

Some people are of the opinion that colleges and universities are free to do anything they want to do as long as their actions are in keeping with the laws and ordinances of the Federal, State and City governments. Such is not the case.

There are many groups, organizations, associations, etc. that have enough power to control some of the actions of colleges and universities. This could be called accountability of quality control. Some college and university administrators call it undue interference, but the regulation and wishes of many of these outside agencies or groups must be met in order for the institutions to be in good standing. And all of them are actually trying to help the college or university to do a better job so that it can be classified as an institution of high quality.

The regional accrediting agencies are thought to be the best determiners of quality and excellence. They get the institution to make a self-study in regard to specified area of action. These areas of action are determined by the regional council, which is made up of leading and representative educators from within the region. Then after the self-study is completed a committee of peers from other institutions in the region are named by the above mentioned council to visit the institution and check on the accuracy of the self-study, suggestions for improvement, and either accredition or no accredition to the council. The vote of the council on the report is final and this is the status of that institution within that regional accreditor body for the next ten years. This status is very important because other groups will accept this evaluation and base their actions - such as the awarding of funds - on that determination.

This regional accreditation has clout but it also has flaws. The six regional accrediting agencies in this country are doing useful work, but they or someone else might do better.

Regional accrediting agencies should judge institutions on the basis of more than minimum standards. They should develop other standards that would cause the institutions to do more to improve the quality of their efforts. Possibly they should add two other steps to their accreditation process. The present minimum standard practice could denote satisfactory accreditation and the next step could denote superior accreditation, followed by excellent status.

These extra steps could offset some of the criticisms of the accrediting process. More than that they could scrutinize the statement of purpose of the institution to make it more qualitative, and they could make graduation requirements more demanding of students performance.

One other criticism of regional accrediting is that the institutions pay their dues and from this money the evaluations are financed and the regional body can change the standards of accreditation if they think they are getting too tough. Connected with this self-interest in evaluating is that self-studies are required for accreditation, and even though peers from other institutions come in on the final visit and make recommendations some of the peers could have self-interest uppermost in their minds by wanting to be employed at the institution where he is a member of the inspecting committee. And it is only natural for faculty members to "put their best foot forward" when they are doing the self-study at the institution where they are employed. All of this makes the process suspect. For instance, the National Institutional Education Department has a fifteen member National Advisory Committee on accreditation and eligibility. It publishes a list of recognized agencies responsible for accrediting higher education institutions and programs. This list is published annually and is used by the federal government to award grants. This action is designed to overcome the weaknesses of regional accreditation.

Possibly one way of offsetting such suspicion is for regional accrediting bodies to change the method of getting peers to do the visiting of the institution and making the final report by getting consulting firms to do their work. This would call for additional consulting firms and the fees for visiting and making the report would be made more expensive. But the educational professionals for the consulting firms could be found and possibly the additional cost could be picked up by those who are the most critical of the procedure - state and federal governments and foundations.

Accrediting and Professional Groups

There is in existence a Council on Postsecondary Accreditation which represents both regional and specialized accrediting agencies. This council was formed in 1975 and it reviews regularly all recognized accrediting agencies to assure the integrity and consistency of their policies and procedures. This is a good idea, but as yet it does not seem to be exerting much influence.

There are professional accrediting associations in Architecture, Art, Business Administration, Dentistry, Education, Engineering, Forestry, Journalism, Landscape Architecture, Law,

Library Science, Medicine, Music, Nursing, Optometry, Pharmacy, Public Health, Social Work, Theology and Veterinary Medicine. In some professional fields, such as Agriculture and Home Economics, there are professional associations but they do not accredit schools.

Some of these accrediting agencies get very specific in what they demand. For instance, under Teacher Education there is the National Council for Accreditation of Teacher Education. This council has stiffened its standards beginning with the 1988-89 college year. The new standards will require students entering NCATE - accredited programs to have at least a 2.5 college grade-point average and pass a standardized basic - skills test. They will require teacher education departments to report specific information on the quality of instruction students receive. Further, they will require the department to assess the ability of prospective teachers before graduation, and to follow their students through their first year of teaching.

There are many other professional organizations in specialized education that do not accredit programs but are helpful in providing discussion of the issues in the profession.

Other non-specialized educational organizations meet regularly to give leadership for higher education as a whole or various parts of it. These, as the others, are vitally interested in improving the quality of higher education. A listing of these organizations may be found in the Encyclopedia of Associations.

Governmental Groups

Professional accrediting agencies and professional associations have influence in fostering high quality and excellence in higher education, but the people who are now putting the most pressure on higher education are those in government. Federal and state, authorities are calling for more accountability. This applies more to state-supported colleges and universities than to those that are private. The private institutions are feeling some of the pressure when they apply for federal grants and for grants from foundations. Counties and cities have a part in financing higher education. Some cities but not many allocate money to urban colleges and universities, and a few allocate money to state-supported institutions located within city limits.

Most of the money used to finance junior and community two-year colleges comes from counties within the district where the colleges are located. Many of these colleges get some money from state allocations.

State governors and legislators are increasingly calling for accountability from state-supported colleges and universities. The National Governors' Association has a Task Force on College Quality. This Task Force will deal with improving assessment of faculty members and students, and assessing the overall performance of colleges and universities. Some educators are telling governors and legislators that lasting institutional change must come from within the colleges and universities. Many states are facing tight fiscal times and they are looking everywhere for ways to cut expenses to offset less money coming from Washington and to keep from having to raise taxes. According to an article in The Chronicle of Higher Education (Oct. 30, 1985, Vol. 31, Number 9, p. 13) the states appropriated approximately thirty-one billion dollars for higher education during the 1985-86 year.

The States have tremendous control over the state-supported colleges and universities. The Legislators determine the amount of state money that the institutions receive. And the amount received is the major factor that determines the quality of what the colleges and universities offer.

Auditing by state agencies is a control over the institutions of higher learning. It is a control that leads to the improvement of the quality of what is being done in the institutions because it guards against fraud and it enforces good business practices in accounting, purchasing, etc.

State legislators propose an enormous number of laws to regulate state colleges and universities. Governors and heads of state agencies also propose changes. The proposals vary all the way from improving quality to being ridiculous. Two items of this nature will illustrate the point. In South Carolina it was agreed today to delete from the appropriations bill the necessity of state colleges and universities who want to raise tuition over 7.5 percent having to get the approval of the Budget and Control Board, the Commission on Higher Education and the Joint Appropriations Review Committee. In California the voters will vote for or against a measure to set a limit of $80,000 on the salary of the governor and restrict the salaries of other state employees - including university faculty members and administrators - to no more than 80 percent of that amount. The measure would allow exceptions to the salary limits if they were approved by a two-thirds vote of state legislators.

Higher education is experiencing close scrutiny at the federal level. The President and members of Congress are looking everywhere for places to cut expenses so that the national debt can be paid off without having to raise taxes, and many are being made.

The Federal Government has a panel of industrial and academic

4

leaders studying the "Health of U.S. Universities and Colleges".

According to an article in The Chronical of Higher Education
(February 19, 1986, Vol. 31, Number 23, page 16) the federal
government allocated 10.1 billion dollars to higher education in
1984, which was an eight percent increase over 1983. Most of this
money - 56 percent - was given to do research and development.
The remainder of the money went to student assistance, graduate
support, institutional assistance, education, library resources,
aid to disadvantaged, education research and statistics, education
for the handicapped, health research and training, health
professions, arts and bilingual humanities, civil rights and
miscellaneous.

Other Groups

There are 4,063 private foundations in the USA and
approximately 2,200 of them are active in grantmaking. They hold
assets estimated at 51 billion dollars, and in 1983 they awarded
four billion dollars to higher education. (The Foundation
Directory, 9th Edition, The Foundation Center, New York, NY, and
The Chronicle of Higher Education, Jan. 22, 1986, Volume 31,
Number 19, p. 18).

Large corporations are giving an increasing number of gifts
to colleges and universities. Much of this is in the form of
equipment.

Alumni Associations always have worked hard to raise money
for their Alma Maters. One raised over twenty-five million last
year without it being any special campaign.

Religious organizations give financial support to their
colleges and universities. Usually these financial allocations
are small compared with the cost of operating these institutions.

The American Association of University Professors has
influence on many campuses. This organization has a "black list"
of colleges and universities that, in their opinion based on their
standards, have not treated one or more of their professors
fairly.

National unions are active on some campuses. These unions
are looking out for the welfare of college and university teachers
and others who are employed by colleges and universities. Strikes
by these unions can virtually close down institutions of higher
learning until they are settled.

The National Association for the Advancement of Colored
People is the national spokesman for black Americans and other
minorities, and for those who support Civil Rights objectives in
America. This organization and other civil rights groups have

5

been and are influential in promoting integration and access. By "access" they want to do everything they can to make a college education available to minorities.

The National Collegiate Athletic Association has about eight hundred member colleges and universities. Membership is voluntary and open to all after a payment of a fee. The NCAA has considerable control over the program and practices in the member institutions. Fines, probation and the discontinuance of athletic programs can be the result of an institution not complying with the standards of the Association.

Regional athletic conferences are open to institutions by invitation. They have some control over the administration of athletic programs in the member institutions. They can, for instance, disqualify a member institution from being conference champion in a given sport when that institution has not lived up to the standards of the conference.

Many people are of the opinion that anyone can sue anyone for anything at anytime, and an increasing number of lawsuits are being filed against colleges and universities. Just about every college or university president or chancellor has one or more lawsuits on his desk at all times.

Colleges and universities should have fewer lawsuits than they have filed against them because they are supposed to have highly intelligent people heading them and they are eleemosynary institutions. Nevertheless, suits should be filed against them if they are violating human rights. Then, every college and university should keep a close eye on practices by the institution to make sure that human rights are not being violated. Even after doing so, suits will be filed against them by people who want attention or money or by people who want to force change.

Large institutions of higher learning find it necessary to retain an attorney to give advice on how to avoid lawsuits and to handle those that are filed. This is time consuming and expensive and in most cases unnecessary. It takes up much time of the administrators and attorney fees are getting higher at an almost alarming rate. Some state supported institutions have the right and do turn over all lawsuits to the State Attorney General. Some are required to do so. However, the Attorney General has to employ additional lawyers to handle such cases and taxpayers have to foot the bill. The vogue of filing lawsuits has made people who are employed by colleges and universities to be more careful in what they do, and this on the whole improves the quality of what is done, and it is most certainly a control.

The groups mentioned above all contribute in varying degrees to the quality of what is done in higher education. In most cases, they improve the quality of what is being done in the colleges or universities.

The accrediting agencies have control over the institutions if the institutions choose to be accredited. The freedom of the institutions is not curtailed if it chooses not to be accredited. However, an institution that chooses not to be accredited will lose students and faculty, and when either is lost in its entirety, the institution ceases to exist.

It has been said that freedom is lost when money is accepted. This has not been the case in higher education in this country. Not any of the sources mentioned above that furnishes money to higher education controls what is taught in higher education. Some grants are given for specific purposes and in these cases the institution has the right to decline them. This is precisely where the battle looms. Educators say give us the money, but do not tell us what to teach, how to teach it or who is to teach it. Federal government officials, state governors and legislators, church officials, and to some extent foundation officials say we want to know if the money is spent for the purpose for which it was given, and we want to know if you are getting good results from such expenditures, and if you can do the job in the future on less money. Thus, there is a call for greater assessment and the simple truth is that educators will have to make more of such available.

Most of this money received by the institutions improves the quality of what is being done in the colleges and universities and on the whole it is not accompanies by control as such. However, those who receive the money will feel kindly toward those who give it and will do whatever they can to please those who give it. Educators should listen to all of them and thank them for their interest and then do what will improve the quality of their product - the graduate.

The other groups mentioned above are pointing in the direction in which they think colleges and universities should move. Most of these suggestions are helpful in improving the quality of higher education.

Therefore, the fight or battle for educators and for our nation is to keep on getting the money that is needed to do high quality work in the colleges and universities and for those who allocate the money not to control what is being done in higher education but to get better assessment reports.

Thus, after getting the money that is needed and getting it without control the problem of quality control becomes an inside affair. Even accreditation is a result of what is being done within the college or university.

So now attention must be given to the entire operation inside the college or university. The following chapters of this book will do this in such a way as to show how high quality and excellence can be obtained from effective social organizations of high quality components. However, the battle to "hold the line" is not entirely over because in some situations individual trustees want to step inside the institution and run it yet they have not been elected to head the institution, and some over zealous alumni want to run the intercollegiate athletic program. Also, some people in business try to get an advantage so that they can make more money off the institution's business operations or off the students and employed personnel. Evidently the head of an institution of higher education is destined to be not only an educator - the leader of the organization of high quality components - but also a tight-rope walker.

It appears that a new concept has to characterize higher education in the future. The concept of "We Must Be Free" will have to be replaced with "Freedom Within More Quality Control and Accountability."

Chapter 2

STRUCTURE

This chapter includes a discussion of the board of control, the president, and the organization.

Controlling boards have various titles, such as board of trustees, board of regents, etc. Such boards will be referred to as boards of control.

The person who is in charge of a junior college, senior college, or university will be referred to as president, even though at some institutions such a person carries the title of chancellor.

Board of Control

The board of control elects the president of the college. The selection of the president of the college or university is the most important function of the board of control. The president, therefore, is the funnel through which all of the desires of the board are presented to the college and through which the desires of the college personnel are presented to the board. Often the president has to stimulate and shape the desires of both groups. More often he has to be the leader in finding the means to realize the desires that are approved. The welfare and future progress of the college depends more on the work of the college president than on any other person connected with the college in any way.

There is much room for improvement in the selection of college presidents. Lay boards often proceed without professional advice to select presidents and often the results are far from desirable. Professional advice on this matter is available from church, state, regional and national educational organizations, and such services should be used by search committees and boards of control.

The qualifications needed for the successful administration of a college are numerous, and will vary with the type and size of the institution and with the particular needs of the institution at any given stage of development. However, the basic qualities are health, ability, training, and experience.

The president's responsibilities are numerous and never ending. He must be a person in good health who is vigorous and who has stamina. Age is not a major factor as long as he has the other qualifications, except it should be reasonable to expect him to continue to have these qualities for the length of time that his services as president are needed. Every person chosen for a presidency should be given at least five years of service in such a position and as long thereafter as his services are advancing the institution to the satisfaction of the board. The board members hear reports indirectly in regard to the effectiveness of the president from other groups, such as the faculty, students, alumni, etc., all of whom must be pleased to a reasonable extent. After evaluating these opinions, the members of the board must make up their minds in regard to the effectiveness and retention of the president.

There is no adequate substitute for brains in higher education and the need for brains applies to the position of president of the college even to a greater extent than to any other person connected with the college because the president of the college has greater responsibilities than any other person employed at the college. This does not mean that the college president must have more brain power than any member of the faculty or any member of the board, but he must have sufficient mental ability to handle his problems effectively and hold the respect of faculty members and all others who are interested in the college.

The president's ability must be more than mental. He must have leadership ability. He must have the ability to work effectively with the students, faculty, alumni, board, and the public. This means that he must be able to cause them to think and plan and work as harmoniously as possible toward the goals of the college.

A misconception in higher education is to think that a person who is not specially trained for college administration can do the job as well as those with such training. Such a notion is in the same category as calling on an attorney rather than a surgeon to perform an appendectomy. It does not necessarily follow that a person specifically trained for college administration can do the job better than a person without such training. The person with such training conceivably might not have the other qualifications that are needed for the job. Possibly the reason why search committees often overlook the professionally trained person in college administration is because higher education has been too slow in offering a program of study for college administrators. In defense of higher education it should be said that over the centuries until rather recently, not many positions in the administration of higher education were available. In earlier days faculties of colleges and universities made more administrative decisions than they do now, and in those days enrollments were small and life was not as segmentized and frustrating as it is today. Now many of the leading colleges and universities offer excellent training in college administration, and there is no excuse for search committees to overlook these important sources to see if they can find a person with such training who has the other qualities that are required for the position.

Experience in college administration is a desirable qualification for the person who is chosen to be a college president. Higher education is now so widespread that many people have had successful experience as vice-presidents, dean,s registrars, etc., and these people should be considered for college presidencies.

It should be remembered that any person chosen for the presidency of a college who has not had specific training in college administration and who has not had some experience in college administration will have to be given sufficient time--the amount depending upon the degree of his deficiencies--to study the field and during that time the institution is bound to regress, mark time, or at least not make adequate progress.

The board of control approves or disapproves the other personnel of the college as recommended by the president of the college.

In addition to choosing the president of the institution, it is the responsibility of the board to approve the personnel employed by the institution. A most important principle of higher education is that the board should approve for employment only the personnel who are recommended by the president of the institution. This does not relegate the board to being a rubber stamp. It is the responsibility of a board member to call to the attention of the president of the institution anything that he believes would be detrimental or helpful to the institution concerning any prospective employee who is recommended. Then it is the responsibility of the president of the institution to check it out, and then report his findings to the individual board member or to the board as a whole. Then the institutional president can stand by his recommendation or withdraw it. Sometimes this will come to a showdown at the board meeting and then the institutional president will either win or lose. If he loses, he will have one employee who will feel that he is directly responsible to the board and not to the institutional president. The institutional president does not need even one such person but if he finds that he has many, he may just as well realize that he has lost his effectiveness and then-it is time for him to look for employment somewhere else.

Even more dangerous than the employment of new personnel is the reemployment or retention of existing personnel. It is the duty of board members to find out what the public thinks of what the institution is doing, and in so doing inevitably someone will have some criticism of some professor or some other employee who did something that the citizen did not like, and in some cases he

11

will insist that the board member see that it is corrected. Some board members tell such people to take it up with the institutional president, which is really the best answer. Some board members take such complaints directly to the institutional president and some take it up in board meetings or board committee meetings.

The institutional president wants to hear such complaints, and also he wants to hear the compliments so that he can evaluate them and take action accordingly.

The crunch comes when some board member wants some person who is employed by the institution and is not recommended for reemployment to remain on the payroll or receive a higher salary, and takes it up with the board in some cases without talking it over with the institutional president and in other cases when he does not get what he wants after talking it over with the institutional president, he tries to run his wishes through the board.

Another side of the issue, and this is far more dangerous, comes when some employees--usually a member of the teaching staff--is recommended to have his contract renewed and some board member wants him fired because he--the board member--does not agree with some point of view that the teach has expounded either in the classroom or elsewhere. This is a "freedom-of-speech" matter and it is jealously guarded by the teaching profession and the accrediting agencies. Board members must realize that the basic purpose of a university is to search for the truth and in doing so different people will see different sides of it and usually a consensus of the various points of view is as close to the truth as can be gotten at any given time. Therefore, there must be tolerance realizing that a faculty member's colleagues are jealous of their profession and they will not tolerate a colleague very long who is consistently off base.

Further no student or anyone else has to accept any given point of view expressed by any teacher. The teacher's point of view must be returned to the teacher on the test or examination but no one has to believe it. Students, as a rule, are attracted by the sensational utterances and acts of teachers, but students are brighter than they often appear and than many people believe, and most of them do not fall for unsubstantiated notions. Students have not had the experience to be pragmatists, but the majority of the students are eclectic in that way put together various points of view in arriving at what they believe.

The board of control approves the general policies under which the institution operates. The state constitution, legislative statutes, or charters clearly fix the authority and responsibility for the operation of the institution of higher learning on the board of control. Board members are representatives of the people who are interested in having the college or university serve their needs or the needs of their descendants. Rarely is a board member an educator and seldom does a board member desire to be employed by the college. Although there are instances to the contrary, no board member should be employed by the college because as a board member he would be sitting in final judgment on his own effectiveness as an employee of the college. The college must be operated in such a way as to please at least a majority of the members of the board. The reason for pleasing the board is that the college was brought into existence to serve a special purpose and the board members must see that such objectives are being pursued in a satisfactory manner. This must be done in order to retain the charter or, in the instance of a state institution, to keep the legislature or the people by way of a constitutional amendment from taking action to discontinue the educational institution.

One way in which the board determines that the college is pursuing its purpose is to establish general policies within which the college is to function. For instance, the board will determine, after receiving recommendations from the college personnel through the president of the college, which degrees will be offered and in which fields of work.

Boards differ on the extent to which they participate in policy making. The author of this volume published a book on policy making in 118 selected colleges of various types. Policy making is a cooperative venture involving trustees, administrator, faculty members, alumni, and students. The type of subject on which a policy is needed usually determines which people are called upon to determine or suggest the policy to the board through the president of the college for adoption.

The board has the right to have all policies relating to the operation of the institution presented to it for adoption or rejection. However, boards usually desire to determine the broader or more general policies and leave to the college personnel, under the leadership of the president, to determine and adopt specific policies on less important matters.

Each board should tell the president the extent to which it desires to participate in determining policies and what types of policies should be presented to the board for adoption or rejection.

A study of board policies of the past keeps some contemporary leaders from making the same error or mistake twice. We should learn from the past but we must not let the past completely control the present. Conditions change and what was good for the past in any given situation might not be good for the present.

Policies must change to keep abreast and ahead of changed conditions.

One major shortcoming of having board members approve all general policies is that some board members who are graduates of the institution would like for the institution to be exactly like it was when they were students there. Such would be a mistake regardless of how effective the institution was when those board members were enrolled there. The reason, of course, is that conditions have changed and present-day students must be prepared to meet the challenges of today and tomorrow and not of yesterday--the past.

This is not to say that some of the attributes of the institution in the past are not good for the institution today, but for it to try to duplicate any given time period in the past would be a definite mistake if not a calamity that would cause the institution to fold up. However, it is almost impossible to kill an institution of higher learning. They seem to have more than nine lives. This is primarily because of the loyalty of alumni and alumnae.

The use of the word "general" in the above principle was intentional and important. If a board attempts to prescribe every detail concerning the operation of an institution of higher learning it is attempting to do something for which they are not prepared, and which will hamstring the administration of the institution to the extent that it will not be able to operate effectively.

The board of control approves a budget as recommended by the president of the college or as changed by the board. The board of control should exercise close supervision of the financial aspects of the institution. Monthly or periodic financial reports should be made to the board on the condition of every phase of the college's activities. Outside auditors should be engaged at lease annually to check on all of the financial transactions and their reports should be made to the board, the president of the college, and to the chief financial officer of the college.

The board of control should give careful attention to the financial holdings of the college. All monies received by the college should be invested or used properly and a complete accounting of such should be made to the board.

The question of how much money is available for the annual operation of the college should be made by the board. The president should be requested to bring in a budget within the available amount. The president will consult with the personnel in the college and do his best to determine the wisest way in which to use the available money. The objective is to get a dollar's worth for every dollar spent and they should be spent for the greatest need that will do the most to cause the institution to achieve its goals.

Every budget should have some flexibility in it. This will make it possible for administrators to adjust to minor changing conditions or unforseen conditions without having to take every minor detail to the board for approval prior to action on the matter. The board members can see these adjustments in the monthly or periodic reports and if such adjustments are in any direction that displeases the board, the president can be so informed, and then he will not permit such changes in the future.

Board of control members should help the institution of higher learning raise money. A major responsibility of a board member is to help raise money for the institution. Often in the case of private universities, board members get seated because of their past gifts or prospective gifts to the university.

A university president cannot raise the amount of money needed all by himself. As a matter of fact, some university presidents are not very good at raising money. At any rate, the university would be a lost cause without the influence of board members in raising money.

Private universities must raise money from individuals, corporations, foundations, and the government. Public universities must get money out of the legislature and now most universities have foundations, and for such the public universities attack the same sources as do the private universities. And in return, the private universities try, and some succeed, in getting money from the state legislatures.

The key to getting money for higher education is to get those who have it or who are in control of it to want to let you have it. That is a very simple statement, but it works even in some cases if they do not have the amount of money that you want. Legislatures can find a way if they want to do something. Private individuals have friends who they can influence to part with the money.

Just how to get them to want to let you have the money is a most complicated phenomenon. Basic to all of it is that the institution must be doing a good job in educating students. Such comes from a qualified faculty. The next point is that the management of the institution must be good. To most business people this means that the institution is not wasteful; it is efficient; and it gets excellent returns on the dollars spent. Then there is the point of getting all of this across to the people who have the money. This is a publicity or marketing job, which is a full story within itself.

15

To have powerful people who will fight for you is extremely important in getting money. A key legislator who believes in the high quality of your work and who is convinced that your operation is exceedingly efficient can get results if he is motivated to do so. The motivation can come from his admiration for the university president, but in all probability it will come from the legislator's desire to be reelected! Possibly his mother or father or both graduated from the university and his motivation comes from that source. The same can be said for a board member of a private university or a public university.

But when a person accepts an appointment as a member of a board of control of an institution of higher learning, he should be ready to raise money for that university.

The board of control should not be politically controlled. Governors of states usually appoint members of boards of control of public colleges and universities. Usually these appointments must be approved by the state senate. No state should permit any governor to have enough appointments during his term of office whereby he would have a majority of the members of the board as his appointees. Higher education should not be controlled by state or federal entities because if they are, they could become centers of incompetent employees trying to teach controlled thought. Such is the opposite of scholarly search for the truth, which is the overall objective of higher education.

Board members, as well as professionals and employees in higher education, should not take themselves quite as seriously as they have in the past. Of course, what they are doing is serious business, but even these people do not know all of the answers. Some board members, for instance, do not know even how to sit on a board! Board members should not try to do everything for the college or university. It is not their job to administer it. That is the job of the administration. All people are human and make mistakes, and we should laugh at ourselves when we make them, but the same mistake must not be made again, and people connected with colleges and universities should keep a sharp eye out for principles and follow them, and see that others do the same.

Yes, it is essential to have a board of control. It helps in seeing that the institution is moving in the direction of the objectives of the college or university. It can interpret the reactions of the constituencies to the administrators. It can get public opinion and financial support for the institution. It can order the president to do what he thinks should be done but does not want to shoulder the repercussions!

Board of trustees, board of regents, etc. but board of control was chosen for this discussion. It was chosen because it

16

has the authority and the responsibility to control the institution. This control is designed by institutional charters and legislative enactments to produce quality. Therefore, all of the above can be classified as quality-control, and when it is done as stated above it improves the quality of the institution.

President

The president of the college or university should be the final authority in administering the institution within the board of control's policies. The responsibilities of a college or university president are enormous, and to carry them out successfully he must have authority to do so in keeping with his responsibilities.

The board of control must back up the president of the institution in the decisions that he makes as long as such are within the board of control's policies. Otherwise, the institution president would be ineffective and become merely a figurehead. He would lose the respect of the people within the college nd those outside. His life would be miserable and it would be time for him to resign.

The president must spend much of his time making decisions. The decisions that he makes should be clean-cut and stated as clearly, sympathetically, and diplomatically as possible, and they should be made as quickly as possible.

Some presidents try to respond to all inquiries within a day to a week. If a question or inquiry has to do with board policy or established institutional policy or the institution's long-range plan or with the president's own philosophy of education, an answer can be given within twenty-four hours. However, other inquiries such as some of those having to do with off-campus controls as described in the first chapter of this volume, can be recognized by letter or telephone within a day to a week with the promise that an answer will be given at the earliest possible date.

To receive a decision within the short period of time presupposes that the president will be in his office at the time that the request for the decision arrives and he will not be tied up in conferences or committee meetings. Chances are that he will not be available immediately, but at least the acknowledgement letter can still go out.

Early recognition is a courtesy that conveys efficiency and the idea of caring. People like this kind of treatment and it gives them the idea that the institution is of high quality, which may not be correct. However, it is a piece of the mosaic that will determine whether or not the institution is of high quality.

17

A president is not an army general. He might feel like one, but certainly he should not act like one. Of course, he should be firm and fair in his decision making and the least he can do is to show some sympathy if his decision is in the negative and he can try to be diplomatic in his response. Some presidents claim that they do not have time to do all of that, but it pays off in the long run, and it would be better for him and the institution for him to delegate some more of his responsibilities to others and take time to be as diplomatic as possible.

Communication is extremely important in the office of the president. Some people literally jump at the opportunity to misinterpret a statement or a decision, especially if it is not the decision he desires. For this reason alone it behooves a president to state his decisions as clearly as he can in plain English. To do such is not easy for many highly educated people. However, a president of a college must realize that his job is not only to communicate with his colleagues, but it is also a job to communicate effectively with the average citizen in order to get the support that his institution must have in order to thrive.

A president of a college must merchandise his product effectively. Here we get into public relations on the part of the president. It will vary with the type of institution, the needs of the institution, and the public relations ability of the president, but it could be said that the president must give approximately one-third of his time to speaking engagements and making public appearances both on and off the campus.

If a product is of value, it is good, but if it is not known, it will not reap maximum benefits. Let us assume that the students who the institution graduates are of high quality and the research work of the faculty members and the services rendered by the institution are also of high quality. If this be the case, the president should tell all the people who will listen to him about their accomplishments. This is merchandizing the product which will result in an even greater following, loyalty, and respect.

On-campus speaking and appearances by the president should be informational and motivational.

Both the large universities and the small colleges at one time or another have a breakdown in communication. Usually we think the more we know about each other and what we are doing, the more understanding we have, and thus the better we like each other or at least the more peace that is apparent or that really exists. This is not always the case but it is worth a try. A part of the president's job is to see that it works. His speeches and appearances on campus should be directed toward this end. Even if

18

a president does not have an attractive personality or even if he is disliked for something or some things he has done in the past, his speeches and his appearances on campus can explain his previous actions and show that he really cares about the students, faculty, and the institution. He can rely a little bit on the power of his office. Some people still hold the office of the presidency in high regard and some still like the touch of the flesh which comes in a good handshake. Some presidents are drunk with the power of the presidency, but soon they get fired or they get that knocked out of them or they come to realize the truth, and that is that the president really does not have much power. Really he is a leader who is there to inspire people to do their best.

Off-campus speeches and appearances are to promote the institution and to render civic service and to advance professionally.

A president of a college is looked up to as a leader--at least until he proves that he is otherwise. This means he should accept some assignments in civic life. He should be a leader in the community or city in which the institution is located. He should not expect to hold offices without doing some work and such work takes time. Directorships and memberships locally should be cherished, for they help in creating better town and grown relationships.

Civic work should extend beyond the local community or city. It should be statewide, regional, national, and if possible worldwide. It helps the institution for the president to be governor of his service club's district or a director for a statewide, national, or worldwide philanthropic enterprise.

A president should participate in and give speeches and hold offices in appropriate professional organizations. By doing such he is giving prestige to the institution that he represents and he is improving his own professional reputation. This is important because the tenure, which is not tenure, of college presidents in any given institution is entirely too short!

The president of the college must be the leader in raising money for the college.

Raising money is an everyday, every-year affair. It is forever! It is one of the most disappointing and rewarding undertaking in existence. Usually it is not an overnight project. It requires planning, patience, persistence, and salesmanship.

The president can have a vice-president for external affairs and a large staff under him whose duty, among other things, is to raise money. Raising money is so difficult that often this group will spend most of its time on "the other things." And the president will be held accountable if this group does not produce the money. But there are times when this group does not produce the money. But there are times when this group cannot produce without the active participation of the president. Therefore, the president must spend approximately one-third of his time planning for and actively engaging in the raising of money. Of course, the amount of time required for the president to spend in doing this kind of work will vary with the type of institution and the particular needs of the institution at any given time.

As mentioned above, board of control members should help raise money. The president of the college should work with them to see that they do so. This is not an easy task. Here the president is working with those who can terminate his services. Therefore much tact must be used in getting this job done. No pressure can be put on a board member for an extended period of time. It has to be persuasion.

Presidents of public institutions must work with members of the legislature to get support money and money for physical facilities. Other members of the administrative staff can do some of this work, but there is no voice as persuasive as the voice of the president if he is held in respect.

Individual donors and foundations like to deal with presidents. Much of the legwork can be done by others, but the president must give much of his time to giving the endeavor the final, climatic punch which often is the difference between success and failure.

Obtaining federal grants will take up much of the president's time, even though much of it is done by outstanding professors and by staff members. Such requires the encouragement and insistence of the president to get the job done.

The most important part of a president's job is to work with students, faculty and administrators primarily in the area of setting high standards of performance for the entire institution and to see that they are met by everyone. This will take approximately one-third of the president's time. But it is the crucial third because without this record of qualitative achievement the president would have little to include in his speeches, and his efforts at raising money would be to no avail because the product that he would be trying to sell would be known as one of little or inadequate value.

The president of the college or university has the opportunity and the responsibility to have more power than anyone else to control the quality of what is done at the institution. He must approve or disapprove the personnel employed by the institution, the degrees that are awarded to students and the contracts and agreements made by the institution. The standards by which these determinations are made largely defines the quality of the institution.

Organization

Empire building is the objective of the private enterprise system. The person in charge is usually trying to figure out how to build a higher pile of whatever it is he is dealing with which in turn will constitute a higher pile of money. A by-product of this that has carried over into every phase of our work life is the effort to build a larger organization. Higher education has not escaped the temptation to try to get more money every year and to enlarge the institution's organization, i.e., administration, almost every year. In an effort to become bigger and better every year often the word "better" is slighted or forgotten altogether.

The heads of many colleges and universities want larger organizations, not necessarily to get the job done well, but to add to their own prestige. They want to appear more powerful. They want more people over whom they have control, and the more administrators he has, the less work he himself has to do because he can construct his organization in such a way that most of them will not be reporting directly to him.

All of such empire building is sheer nonsense and a waste of money.

There has been a tendency in higher education to give high-sounding titles to administrators. Such has been copied from business and industry, and one might expect higher education, with plenty of words, to lead the way in such foolishness.

Beware of high-sounding titles anywhere. They could be psychological props to offset or placate deserved raises in salaries. They could be screens to give the people more money than they deserve. They could disguise an unneeded enterprise. At any rate, administrators are employed to serve and the title is supposed to or should indicate the service he is to render, and this in higher education and elsewhere should be understandable to the people who are paying for the service.

Organization in institutions of higher education should be just enough and no more than is needed to get the job done well. When the word "well" is used, it leaves the gate open for packing the deck. However, an illustration of what is meant by doing a job well is the following. One function of a registrar obviously is to register students. He should be held responsible for getting the job done accurately and courteously in the shortest period of time with the minimum, if any, of inconvenience to the students, faculty, and other administrators. He must do it in keeping with national and state laws, boards and institution policy, and the policies of his own office. He must report his results immediately to his immediate superior. He should summarize the reactions of the students, faculty, and other administrators to his operation and with such, make changes or recommendations for his own staff and himself concerning policies and procedures that could improve the operation for the future.

Some people think the bigger the organizational chart, the more important and the better it is. Bigger, of course, is not necessarily better. Many small things are equally as effective.

Of course, there should be enough organization in higher education to distribute responsibility and authority in such a way as to have an efficient operation in keeping with established policies.

Computerization has contributed to efficiency in higher education and it should have cut down on the number of employees in administration, but generally speaking it has not. This is one of the reasons why cost efficiency has not been achieved in higher education as a whole.

Efficiency and effectiveness are the key words in organization.

Effectiveness is the more important, but usually it cannot be achieved without efficiency.

Organization should be goal-oriented. It should be the means toward achieving the established and changing goals of the institution. The established goals that do not change very often are those stated in the charters and statutes that founded the institution. Usually these are stated in general terms. The goals that change are of two types. One type has to do with the changing needs of the institution's constituency. The other has to do with new or changed requirements of the board of control, governmental agencies, accrediting agencies, etc.

The organization of the institution must be flexible enough to meet the needs of all of these goals. This means that organization must take into consideration the interests, abilities, and the adaptability of the presently employed administrators and those who can be obtained. Sometimes personal philosophies and ambitions of currently employed administrators interfere with changing duties to meet new or changed needs. Some such people have to be fired, reassigned, or circumvented. To work around them is expensive because usually they are contributing virtually nothing to the ongoing institution. But sometimes it is wise to do so. The person could be near retirement. He could have meant so much to the institution in the past that to fire him would not only infuriate him, but also alienate many other people. The purpose of administration is not to make friends. It is to have goal-oriented efficiency and effectiveness, but this cannot be achieved when those who are trying to do it have too many enemies.

Some organizations are so authoritative in nature that they mitigate against a flow of ideas from anyone. Ideas for the realization of the goals of the institution should come from all sources--the students, faculty, administrator, staff, alumni/ae, townspeople, and other citizens. The cooperation, knowledge, and experience of all concerned can make the institution come closer to realizing its goals. This is especially true among the administrators because they see each other more often and meet more often and really are more concerned than any other group in the overall achievements of the institution.

Administrators should welcome the opportunity to shift around and accept new duties if they feel or are competent to administer them because this gives them additional experience in other phases of higher education. This is advantageous for them because the broader the background, the more knowledgeable the person is and such is desirable or required of the person who is in the top position. Of course, some people do not want to accept the responsibilities that go with the presidency of an institution of higher learning, but higher education needs more presidents who have a track record of achievement in the broad areas of college and university administration.

An effective organization is one that will contribute the maximum in benefits for the students. What can the administrators do to help students learn more? The duties of administrators should be designed to achieve this objective.

An organization is efficient when it turns out only necessary reports and work on time. Reports have to be made to boards of control and practically everyone else, and these must be made by the date that they are due. Much information is ground out especially by computers that are not needed and not used. Such is a waste of money. However, wise decisions must be based on facts and these must be made available prior to the time that the decisions must be made.

It is one thing to assume that people know what they are supposed to do, but this is not always the case. There is no adequate substitute for a manual of duties. Some administrators think that such should be only for staff people and in the form of job descriptions. This is not correct. Administrators need them as much as anyone else to keep them from being freewheeling big shots accomplishing nothing. Of course, these manuals of duties cannot remain entirely static. There must be continuous review and revision of the duties in keeping with changing needs of the constituency and the effectiveness of the individual and his assistants or staff.

Now it is one thing for a person to know what he is supposed to do and it is another thing to get him to do it. All administrators should feel dedicated and responsible, but some do not. Some administrators are good at supervising the work of others, but some are not. Some administrators will follow institutional policies and others will not. Some administrators function on the premise that anyone will be permitted to do anything that he wants to do. This either consciously or unconsciously is designed to win friends, but at the same time it destroys standards. Such opportunism should not be tolerated.

Every person in administration should be supervised by his superior, including the president of the institution. The board of control should supervise the president as it does by getting reports from him and asking him questions at board meetings. The president should supervise the vice-president or vice-presidents and right on down the line everyone within the organization should be supervised periodically to see that he is performing his duties satisfactorily. If he is not performing them satisfactorily, he should be told in no uncertain terms what and how he should change his action. Such firmness is rough on love and friendship, but it results in respect. Institutions of higher learning are built on respect.

One certain way in which to save money, or cut expenses, is to have as few people as possible in support positions and have as few as possible with high-ranking titles. Sometimes this cannot be done immediately because some of these people have given long years of good service to the institution, but through attrition and a freeze on further additional jobs, much can be done to cut expenses.

Every institution has an organizational chart. Every chart should have on it someone designated as Quality Control Coordinator, who will be directly responsible to the president. The president can do this in the smaller institutions, but someone else will have to do the leg work in the larger institutions. The coordinator should work with all groups on or off the campus that are in the process of setting up or changing standards, qualifications or criteria for any part of the institution. Then when the proposed standards get to the president through established channels the coordinator can make his recommendations to the president for his approval, denial, or modification. In order not to add another administrator to the payroll, the duties of the coordinator may be added to those carried by the assistant to the president or the executive vice president.

Chapter 3

FINANCE AND PLANNING

This chapter will consider money and budget, fund raising and planning.

Money, Accounting, and Budget

How much money is available or can be made available for the operation of the institution? This is one of the controlling factors in determining how well the objectives of the institution can be realized. The other major factor is the insight ability and performance of those who are charged with the responsibility of planning and carrying out the program.

An analysis of the income from the various sources during the past five or ten years can give the base on which to make extrapolated forecasts. Such within itself is about as reliable as weather forecasts. Each and every source of past income must be assessed for future productivity. Will the size of the student body be generally the same, larger or smaller? Will the money from the state or church, etc., be generally the same, more or less? Will the money received from grants change? Will contributions to the endowment change? Will interest on invested money change? Will inflation increase? Such are the basic questions that must be answered based on the best information that can be obtained from experts inside or outside the institution. The answers to these questions are too important in the life of the institution to leave to a president or a chief financial officer or even to a board of control.

Then what efforts by the institution to raise or lower income will be taken during the next year or next few years? Will an effort be made, with likelihood of success, to increase the size of the student body thus increasing income? Will tuition be raised or lowered? Can more money be obtained from the state, church, federal grants, etc.? Can more money be raised for the endowment?

In most businesses the major alternative to rising costs of operation or production is to pass the increased cost on to the customer. Of course, the objective in doing so is to shave the increased cost as closely as possible so that the price of the product is lower than that of the competitor's. If this is not done, the demand for the product dwindles or stops and the market has been lost unless the quality of the product is better than that of the competitor's and the consumer is willing to pay the difference. As the cost of living increases, more and more people are choosing the cheapest article even though some of them would prefer to have the article of better quality.

Higher education is passing some of the increased cost on to the consumer by raising the price of tuition, board, and meals. However, higher education is reluctant to sit back and say that it will simply pass the increased cost on to the consumer, because they are of the opinion that such will cause the prospective consumers to choose not to buy their products. It is not known how accurate this assumption is today. It is true that if any given institution raises its prices considerably higher than most of the other institutions, enrollment will fall off unless, like the better product mentioned above, that institution has a much better reputation for quality than the others. However, what would be the outcome if all of the institutions would raise their prices at the same time is not known. Possibly it would work and be the answer, but no one seems to be ready to organize such an undertaking.

Rather than that, some institutions are turning to other rather radical means of financing. Some are rather heartbreaking for those who are employed by the institutions or who are graduates. The more recent actions have been to sell off a part of the campus and to drastically reduce the number of professors employed. These are last-ditch alternatives and the latter could cause the institution to get into trouble with the accrediting agencies since some of the professors being fired or let off are those with tenure. If such takes place, such institutions could have to close their doors in the very near future.

Evidently it is time for higher education--both private and public--to experience some new ideas in financing. Possibly a national commission composed of higher education officials and leading representatives of the financial world should give careful thought to discovering new ideas for financing higher education that will be acceptable to colleges and universities.

Excellent accounting is as important in higher education as it is in any other enterprise. The system used varies with institutions, but all of them account for every penny received and every penny spent. Monthly, bi-monthly, weekly, or even daily reports are made so that monitoring can be done to make certain that all are living within the budget and the institution is operating within its income. Cost accounting in particular is increasingly important in institutions of higher learning because these institutions are being increasingly called upon to be more accountable. Accountability has been and is and should be an important emphasis in higher education.

There is no substitute for outside audits of all financial records in the institutions. This includes the financial records of student organizations. All people connected with the

26

institution should know the outcome of the annual audits. Such gives all greater confidence in the institution, and avoids embarrassing and even criminal situations.

It is exceedingly difficult to accurately estimate income and expenses a year in advance. But to come out in the black is one of the major criteria on which the head of an institution is judged. The writer received word yesterday that the president of a certain college resigned, and his resignation had to do with a financial deficit situation. Of course, the budget is approved by the board of control and is often changed by the board, but even after that the board seldom blames itself if the institution does not come out in the black at the end of the year. The board of control blames the head of the institution. If errors of judgment are made and some budgeted expenditures are cut or eliminated during the year, again the head of the institution is blamed by faculty, staff, students, and/or alumni/ae.

Budgeting expenditures for a year in advance is a tough job. Cost accounting is a must in the process. Which courses, departments, schools, services brought in as much money as they spent last year? How much money have they requested for next year? Do we have reason to believe they will bring in as much money next year as they have requested? Which segments of the institution that were not cost-effective last year give promise of being cost-effective next year? It takes time for some segments to become cost-effective. And sometimes uncontrollable circumstances cause a few segments not to produce during a given year. Which of the segments can be curtailed or eliminated for next year without seriously hurting the institution? Which new segments should be added to meet the needs of the people in keeping with the objectives of the institution?

The development of a budget is traumatic in that many people do not get what they want. The traditional way in which it is developed will be outlined. The president of the institution gets information from people within the institution concerning how many students are expected to enroll for the coming year. This usually comes from his director of admissions. However, information on the number of present students that would be expected to return for the next year could come from other sources within the institution. This will give the president the information concerning the amount of money that will from students during the coming year. Then from sources outside the institution, the president will find out how much money the institution will get from other sources. For instance, a state-supported college or university will get a certain amount of money from the legislature.

With this information the president usually meets with his vice-president or administrative council and develops guidelines for developing the budget. He needs to find out from them the status of specific programs, the number of professional promotions coming up, the cost (increase or decrease) of support enterprises at the institution, and which of these should be changed. This will result in guidelines to department heads stating the number and classification of students to expect and the salary and wage increases or decreases to expect.

The department heads throughout the institution then go to work with a copy of their budget for the current year in hand. They should involve all of the members of the department and representative students in determining what they should request for the next year. These proposals are sent to the respective deans. The deans send them on to the vice-presidents with their comments. The vice-presidents take them up with the president, either at a meeting or individually. Necessary adjustments are then made with the president making the final decision. The president takes the budget to the board of control for final approval.

The business office monitors the budget to see that the departments live within their budgets. Expenditures are stopped when they use up all of the money in their budgets, unless the dean can transfer some money from one item to another within his school or college or unless additional funds can be obtained from some other source.

Lately there have been some new ideas developed in budget making.

One such idea is called the "zero-base" form for budgeting. This approach causes each unit to start from zero and justify its existence each year. Each unit must reexamine its objectives, priorities, etc., and come up with three proposals--one is a minimum, another is maintenance, and the other is desired.

Another approach is called "formula budgeting." Such formulae are usually based on enrollment data and credit-hour production. This is translated into full-time equivalency (FTE) and the number of faculty positions required is based on this FTE. The formula also takes into consideration clerical support, supplies and equipment, library, physical plant maintenance, research, public service, general administration, etc. This approach applies very well to instruction, but it is not as applicable when it is applied to research and public service.

Getting the most out of a dollar that is possible is the name of the game. Of course, it must be done in an honest way without exploiting anyone. Shrewd business management in higher education is essential, and for some institutions it will be the reason for survival.

Excellent business administration is a must in higher education. It gives people inside and outside of the institution a good feeling when they know that no one is running off with any of the money that belongs to the institution. These same people are pleased when they see that purchasing is done in keeping with regulations and with a full understanding of the value of the dollar. These are only two of the valued services that a business office contributes to the well-being of a college or university. With the use of computers the business office can turn out endless numbers or figures which serve two very important purposes. These reports can satisfy the desire for accountability as far as numbers go. Those people who like numbers can be flooded with them, and they should get all that they want. The other important function that these reports serve is to let the people within the institution know what everything costs and with this information decisions can be made to place the money where it will be of greatest value in educating the student, and this is Quality Control.

Fund Raising

The head of an institution of higher education must be an effective fund raiser. Throughout the history of higher education in the USA, more heads of institutions have been chosen for their potential to raise money than for any other reason. This has been one of the reasons why higher education has not made any more progress than it has. So many of these people knew very little or too little about education to make decisions to improve scholarship and research, and were too arrogant to leave it to others who knew how. But all of such cannot be delegated to others, and that is the reason why the head of an institution of higher education should be an educator. However, being an educator is not enough. He must be able to raise money.

No one can successfully substitute for the head of the institution in certain fund-raising situation.

One very difficult job for the head of an institution is to get board approval for the amount of money that he wants for his institution when more than his institution is under the same board. This applies to state-supported institutions that are under multi-institution boards or state commissions, and also to church-supported institutions that are under multi-institution boards. Such boards have tremendous power and for any institution to get more than is approved by these boards is virtually impossible and dangerous. Dangerous in that the head of the institution might be removed from his position if he tries or permits his associates to try. About the only way in which he can get away with it is for the amount of extra money to be enough to give all of the other institutions under that board an equally proportionate increase.

29

Battling for funds at board and commission levels usually becomes vicious. Very few boards and commission members will admit it, but much of the outcome of a fight for funds for any given year is determined before the fight begins. A few institutions do not work on it, but most of them work year-round to get friends of the institution appointed or elected to membership on the commission or board. This is as true of church-related institutions as it is of state-supported institutions.

Adroit presentation of the needs of the institution must be made by the head of the institution because often he and he alone from the institution is the only one to whom the board or commission members will listen. Persuasion and the personality of the head of the institution are important. How well-liked is the head of the institution? All of these factors come into the decision, but at a secondary level. At the first level come emergencies that in the opinion of the board members should be corrected. Also at the first level in most cases comes the production of the institution. Usually this is measured by the credit hours produced. But then the major factor comes into play and that is: what has the institution meant to me and to mine? All of this has to do with getting money for operation and for the physical plant as well.

The fight is not really over after the boards and commissions have made their determination. Then comes work with the legislatures and the churches. This work is difficult, but they are the ones with the money.

Work with the legislature is lobbying. Some people call it by other names, but lobbying is what it is.

Some central boards of control prohibit or discourage work by the institution with the legislature, but it goes on in one way or the other.

Even though state-supported institutions draw funds through the state treasurer from all of the tax-paying people of the state, any given institution should and almost must have the support of the county in which it resides. This is difficult and often messy and sometimes serious because some of the local legislators, as well as some legislators from other parts of the state, want to show their power locally by getting the institution to do some favor for them or their friends--like giving a job at the institution to some friend. This "you scratch my back and I'll scratch yours" is not new. It goes on with some board of control members, some governors, and some congressmen. There is only one professional and long-range effective answer and it is that we are glad that you called this person to our attention and we will see that he is given careful and serious consideration. Then it is a must to go ahead and select the best qualified person for the job and report to the legislator accordingly. With such a stand sometimes the requests for favoritism will stop or become less frequent. It is important to follow up a turndown of a legislator with something that will boost his ego, such as public compliments for something that he has done, invitations to functions that will place him in a prominent and favorable position, etc.

Legislators, local and statewide, must be given the facts about the institution's request for operating funds and capital improvements. More than that they should be constantly reminded about these needs. The institution should be visible through the head or some of his representatives when the votes on important higher education issues are taken. A legislator knows that your institution has great influence with many voters and practically every legislator wants to get reelected.

Church politics can get about as rough as state politics. Some deception goes on such as in the case where the minister is prejudiced and claims that it is the will of God for him to vote for or against the measure as the case may be. Of course, some do get close enough to God to make such a claim and to them we say, "More power to you."

Heads of church-related colleges and universities are often asked to speak in pulpits. Some of these invitations are to meet the convenience of the minister, but in other instances the people really want to know about religion in higher education. These are fine opportunities, not only to inform, but also to make friends for the institution.

Student groups are often invited to church services to put on a program of some kind, and it is really good business for a church-related institution to have effective groups to make such appearances. It not only makes the institution better known and like, it is excellent training for the students.

Attendance at church conferences is a must for the church-related colleges and universities. Usually it is not difficult to get placed on the programs at such gatherings, but if not, it is a good time to "collar" people and "sell your bill of goods."

The head of church-related college or university has the opportunity and obligation to work for financial support from the churches through the members of the board of control of that institution. These people have been chose for membership on the board because they are leaders and representative. They have or should have great influence, and not to work with them constantly would be to miss a great opportunity.

Private colleges and universities historically have worked

31

harder or at least given more time than public colleges and universities trying to get money from foundations. This is still true today; however, public institutions are stepping up their work with foundations much to the disdain of private institutions. Older foundations and educational foundations in the past have given more money to private institutions for the simple reason that they do not have the state coffers from which to draw funds.

During more recent years individuals who made a lot of money set up foundations and both private and public institutions have bombarded them with requests for grants.

Even more recently the federal government has made enormous amounts of money available to junior colleges, senior colleges, universities, both public and private. The scramble for these funds has been frantic. These funds have been and are in the form of grants and loans to the institution, to selected faculty members or departments doing research, and to students.

Preparation of grant requests is an art within itself. Usually they have to be innovative, presented by a prestigious institution, presented by a distinguished researcher, or presented by some institution that is known for its religious or racial composition. A few grants have been made to all-male institutions to keep them going. Relatively few have been made to all-female institutions for the same purpose. Most of these single-sex institutions changed over to coeducational institutions with the hope of better qualifying for federal funds.

Courses are in the curriculum of some institutions to teach students how to prepare grant requests. To obtain such funds is so very important that often the reputation of an institution is judged by the amount of money it obtains in grants. The real test in this respect is what the institution produces from these funds, and such is the basis on which the better foundations give consideration to further requests from any given source.

It is not known how grants have changed the direction of higher education in the USA, but they have most certainly had their influence. Some grants have strings attached and some institutions are so very desperate for funds that they accept the conditions rather than state that the conditions are contrary to the objective of the institution. A few institutions have refused to accept grants for that reason.

Getting grant money should be based on the quality of the program for which the grant is requested. Everyone in higher education should work on that assumption for therein lies the essence of higher education without which the institution sooner or later will fail or be relegated to insignificance. The reason why people who do not work on that assumption get away with it, at least for awhile and sometimes longer, is because it is almost impossible to kill an institution of higher education. The reason for this is that the alumni and friends of the institution somehow and in some cases almost miraculously find some way to keep it going in one form or size or another.

Knowing and being respected or liked by those who are in charge of administering grant money is added plus and sometimes the difference between getting it or failing to do so. Cultivation of such people takes endless hours over a period of many years. It should be the sort of thing that goes on continuously even though the heads of the institutions and the people who are in charge of the grants change often. The heads of some institutions know that they must get grant money or they must give up their positions and let others have them.

Practically every senior college and university--both public and private--has a foundation which raises funds from alumni, friends, corporations, and wherever they can get it. Yale University just broke the world's record in raising such funds. The amount that Yale raised in one campaign was three hundred fifty million dollars. This is a private institution and it simply cannot operate without such funds. The alumni know it and they are so very proud of their alma mater that they give generously. Such is not the case with most institutions. It is a year-in, year-out struggle. They go after restricted or unrestricted gifts. They prefer unrestricted gifts which give the administrator the flexibility to put the money where it is needed most, because herein lies the genius of administration. Without such results from these wise investments, in the direction in which the institution should move in order to most effectively realize the objectives of the institution, quality or excellence is not obtained and the institution falls short of its potential.

Innovativeness is important in raising funds for the foundation. Much to the credit of those who have worked and are working in this area all sorts of options are available to the would-be giver. A gift to an eleemosynary institution, and all of them are classed as such, is tax deductible. This option has been worked to the limit. "Remember us in your will" rings in the ears of every conscientious alumni/ae. Living endowments have been stressed by some institutions whereby an alumni or friend promises to give a certain amount to the institution every year for a certain number of years or until the individual notifies the institution that it will be discontinued. Scholarship funds honoring the donor or a favorite person who has or is serving at the institution can be found at practically every institution. Many other approaches are made to prospective donors and fresh new ideas along this line can be seen every year.

Fund raising in private junior colleges follows the same

pattern as mentioned above with the exception of the grants for research. Research is not a function of a junior college, although a few members of such faculties are doing such on their own time with their own funds.

Fund raising at public junior colleges is somewhat different in that they have an additional trough from which to get funds and it is the district in which the institution is located. These districts, consisting of several counties, levy millage for the partial support of such institutions. Increasingly these institutions have been getting state funds. And very importantly these institutions have been getting large grants from the federal government. For instance, the Vocational Education Act has made an enormous amount of money available to public junior colleges for vocational and technical training of students. Public junior colleges enjoy the support of local, state, federal support and the support of industry because the junior colleges prepare students to fill the jobs of industry. Without such trained personnel, industry simply will not locate in the area, and all areas are vitally interested in increasing the per-capita income of their people.

The head of the institution must see that his institution has an adequate staff to raise funds continuously and with continuity. Even with such at times in certain institutions, it is necessary to enter into contracts with outside fund-raising organizations to get the job done. Such firms can look at the institution more objectively and can offer approaches that have proved to be successful in other institutions. Also, such firms can set financial goals that sometimes the head of the institution or the board of control feel that they cannot get away with. It must be remembered, however, that even with such assistance and guidance from fund-raising management firms, the legwork must be done by members of the institutions' staff, alumni, and other local friends. The firms merely tell you how much to try to get, how to go about it, and then for their fee they get a part of the money raised, and this take is not exorbitant.

Having the money does not necessarily mean that any given institution will give students a high quality of education, but without such the students are bound to be shortchanged.

Planning

Vision is necessary in higher education. It is exceedingly helpful when the person with the most realizable vision is the president of the institution. For the president to transmit this realizable vision to others within and outside the institution is the mark of excellent leadership.

The president of the institution must know that planning for the institution must go on by someone or by more than one person on a full-time basis every day throughout every year. The president of the institution must be the leader of the planning by providing direction, but he will not be able to find time to work out the details, and others in the department of institutional research or the department of research and planning must be ready to do it.

It is better for the person who is charged with this responsibility to do the planning to be someone with a background in educational research rather than a person who has had training and experience only in finance. So often people in finance are chosen for such work, but they as a rule lack the philosophical background and knowledge of higher education. They usually try to reduce everything to dollars and cents which of course is very important, but the most important attribute in such work is to know which dollar to save. This gets into value judgments that far exceed cost-effectiveness.

Continuous research, study, and planning at the institution should be directed toward the needs of the constituency in a changing world to make certain that the institution is preparing students to meet the most important needs that properly come within the scope of the institution's purpose.

Goals and objectives of an institution of higher learning are usually printed in the institution's catalog. Originally they came from the charters or statutes that established the institution. Some of these have been amended. Usually these statements of purpose are very general in nature. These objectives have been amplified and defined periodically to meet the changing needs of constituents.

Every institution of higher learning should have a master plan. Some years ago the writer was named chairman of the University Planning Council at Florida State University, and the president of that university requested us to come up with a master plan that would reflect the opportunities and needs of the university for the next fifty years. After meeting once a week for two years, the council came up with a plan, even though it was conceded by the members of the council that in all probability it did not foresee for fifty years. It was gratifying to see how much foresight that council had and put into that master plan.

Planning today is for a much shorter period of time because a much faster changing world is shortening the length of human vision except in extraordinary cases. Master plans projecting for ten years are more appropriate now and every master plan should be reevaluated every year.

A master plan starts with a definition of the institution's

35

constituency or would-be constituency. An analysis of past student enrollment defines constituency. However, this does not necessarily define the constituency of the future. The council should determine the realistic size and needs of the constituency of the future. Would the students of the future come from a radius of one hundred miles from the institution, three hundred miles, the entire state, the state and all contiguous states, the nation, or the world? What percentage of the students would be from nearby? What percentage from other countries, etc.?

At this point a sociological study of the needs of the projected students should be made. For instance, if most of the students would come from the state in which the institution is located and that state was a service state and if most of the graduates of the institution settled in that state, this would be a major clue in determining the types of jobs for which the students should be prepared to perform successfully.

The council should determine the desirable size of the student body for the future. Should it be no more than ten thousand within ten years, or whatever?

The goals and objectives of the university must be the controlling factor in working out the master plan. It is not difficult to connect the needs of the projected constituents to the goals and objectives of the institution.

The next step is to consider the means of realizing these ends. The three traditional areas of higher education are instruction, research, and public service. Some smaller institutions would not be interested in all three of these areas. And those three areas do not encompass all that must be included in a master plan. Others have to do with intercollegiate athletics, extracurricular activities, etc.

The council should give careful consideration to every program and activity in existence at the institution and decide if any of these should be eliminated and what should be added in order to meet the objectives of the institution for the next ten years. This will be the heart of the plan.

At this point a landscape architect is needed. This person should be a member of a firm that has had successful experience in planning college and university campuses. Surely the leading local or nearby landscape architect will want this assignment. That person could be the most qualified person in the nation for it, but in all probability he will not be. It is essential to have a top-notch firm for this job, and this does not mean that he should be from someplace far away. However, the writer had the same landscape architectural firm from thirteen hundred miles away to serve at the university during the entire twenty-five years that he was president of that institution.

The landscape architectural firm will estimate the cost of the proposed new buildings and the renovation of others and the cost of every shrub and tree that is to be planted on the campus. This will accompany the beautiful maps that he will furnish the institution showing the proposed location of every new building and which ones should be demolished and how the grounds should look and where each thing should be placed.

The contract with the landscape architectural firm should cause him to visit the campus every year to meet with the planning council and to be on call for more frequent visits as needed.

The council will need more than the cost of the changes in buildings and grounds. It will need the projected cost of the remainder of the master plan. Here the business officers will be needed. They know the cost of present operations. All they need to do is to look at the audit of last year and the budget for the present year. They will need to adjust such to fit in with any changes included in the master plan and then add to it the projected cost of the proposed additions that are included in the master plan. Of course, if retrenchment is anticipated and included in the master plan, the estimated costs for the future will be less rather than more. Cost accounting will be invaluable at this state of the planning.

It is entirely possible that the business officers will need to call in some consultants to assist them in projecting costs for the next ten years. By the way, consultants will need to be called in when the council is considering other parts of the master plan.

Thus, with an outline of what should be done, a map showing where it should be and the projected cost of all of it, the master plan is intact and ready to be presented to the president of the institution for him to take to the board of control for approval.

The planning council at Florida State consisted of fifteen people--all of the vice-presidents, all of the deans, and the chief finance officer. A planning council should be in existence all of the time. The staff in the Department of Institutional Research and Planning will be working on the master plan continuously and should call meetings of the planning council as needed. It is important to have wide input into the deliberations of the planning for the institution. Each member of the council should see that all people under him, including students, should have opportunities to express their views in some organized way. It is helpful to have hearings on the plans when critical or very important items are under consideration. The major question that the planning council would like for everyone connected with the institution, including the alumni/ae, to keep in mind and respond to is: What should be done in order for this institution to do a better job of what it is trying to do, and what more can this institution do to better serve its constituents and humanity as a whole?

The above approach to planning is the more traditional approach. In recent years, more sophisticated approaches have been developed and are in use on some campuses.

Computer centers have been on many college and university campuses for quite awhile. The writer was directly in charge of a computer center on a university campus and it amazed him to see how much information the center could turn out, and how the computers were no better than the people who were feeding information into them.

The computer centers have made it possible for these new approaches in planning to come into existence.

One such system is called PPBS (planning, programming, budgeting systems) or PB (program budgeting). It breaks away from the traditional input-oriented fiscal-planning methodology to one that is output-oriented. It is designed for planning and budgeting over a period of five to ten years. This system can provide data for decision making in terms of total programs rather than on a departmental basis.

Departments of Institutional Research and Planning should be out front in regard to all developments in higher education. They should be ready to offer assistance in such matters as selection of search committees, job descriptions, rating scales of administrators, equal opportunity goals, evaluation forms of instruction, student evaluation of teachers forms, affirmative action, tenure, collective bargaining, planning for slowdowns, mass call-ins of sickness, picketing, and strikes, etc. They should be well acquainted with management by objectives, management information system, and the like.

These research and planning centers can be of inestimable value to the institution by gathering the facts that point up prolification, duplication, inefficiencies, and cost-effectiveness. These facts can be handed on to higher-ups for their value judgments and action.

Plans cannot always be followed. Some plans should not be followed. Both because of changed conditions or lack of foresight. However, there is a tendency for people to be opportunists and react favorably to just anything that comes along, especially if they come from people in power. Expediency is the best way of characterizing the action of some people. They do what is immediate without any thought as to long-range implications. A plan for the institution is essential because it is based on objectives and principles. This, if adhered to, will offset pressure, opportunists, and action based on expediency only.

No institution should try to be everything to everybody. It should be selective in its program offerings. No institution should put money into buildings and grounds when it is needed for instruction and research. Quality comes from highly competent people not trying to spread themselves too thin.

Chapter 4

PERSONNEL

The first section of this chapter considers the selection and performance of personnel. The second section gives special attention to the faculty. Then there is a section on students followed by a discussion of admission and financial aid.

Selection and Performance

Choosing personnel is the most important function of administrators. Yes, getting money is important, but how it is used depends upon qualifications and performance of the personnel chosen to work at the institution.

There is very little turnover in higher education personnel. Nevertheless, some people change jobs, some retire, and some die, and a few are dismissed even though most faculty members have tenure. This provides an opportunity for administrators, which includes teaching department chairmen, to improve the quality of the institution.

Salesmanship and persuasion have a part in attracting outstanding personnel, but in higher education the salary range, the reputation of the institution, the quality of existing personnel, the cultural opportunities, and health condition of the environment are given greater weight by high-quality prospective personnel.

One question that is often asked in regard to the effectiveness of the head of an institution of higher education is: Has the academic standing of the institution been enhanced during the time that he has been in office? No better question could be asked about an institution of higher education.

The president however does very little of the choosing of personnel. Of course, he has the final approval, subject to the approval of the board of control. Most choices originally are made by teaching department chairmen, search committees, and directors of personnel. These people must know and know unequivocally that the president of the institution has a list of priorities that clearly places the academic or scholastic standing of the institution first, and he surely will not approve anything less. Some deans, vice-presidents, and presidents have sent back to the recommending groups or individuals names of people who in their opinions are not highly qualified enough for the position. This is the way it should be, but often is not. When recommendations are returned asking for others often there is a loud cry saying, for example, "There are only two institutions in this county offering Ph.D.s in this field and they turn out just a few and they have so many high-salaried offers that we can't get them." The answer should be: "Keep trying. We want only one of the good ones."

The tone of the institution is largely determined by the quality of the personnel assembled in any given institution of higher learning. This is true because the student body catches it from the more permanent members of the college or university family--the employed personnel.

The reputation and correspondingly the tone of an institution is usually determined by having employed personnel who really know what they are doing, have an affection or respect or faith in the institution where they are employed, and cooperate with each other to enhance the effectiveness of the institution as a whole.

Therefore each and every employee--including those in the lowest-paid jobs on the campus--should be encouraged to exert or reflect a positive influence on the institution. This means that in choosing personnel every effort should be made to determine whether the person in addition to really knowing how to do the job is capable of being cooperative and loyal. Nothing should take the place of know-how or knowledge and ability to do the job, but after that has been established then these other qualities should be sought.

There is always the danger of choosing the person who will be loyal to the institution or to the person doing the choosing and is not capable of doing high-quality work. This coupled with the choice of people who are unqualified friends of those in power will weaken the reputation of the institution quicker, or at least more surely, than anything else.

All of this is certainly the heart of higher education. For the reputation of the institution draws qualified students, and such students and reputation draw grants, appropriations, and gifts--money.

Some people are of the opinion that professors in particular believe in their subject matter and in that only. They think they are oblivious to the environment in which they are located. Indeed, it often appears that this is true. However, this is not true throughout the working life of these people. At some point in their career most of these people give their own subject and their own professional association first priority even above the institution in which they work. The reason for this is that with their advancement in teaching and/or research in their field, their professional association can be of assistance in getting the individual a better job in some other institution. Rarely does a person's field of work change, but the places in which most of them work change many times.

"Publish or perish" has been a slogan in most universities. This means that those who publish scholarly articles and books get promoted and are awarded tenure. That is the reason why university teachers give so much time to research.

In spite of what has just been said, everything else being equal, and it seldom is, it is better to choose a person for employment who is sympathetic with the objectives of the institution.

Rarely is a person satisfied with a setting in which he is working. Possibly it is good that he is not. For with satisfaction we often have complacency, and complacency is exactly what is not wanted in higher education. Neither is dissatisfaction wanted. Perfection is not possible with a group of independent thinkers and workers, or any other group or individual. But everyone should be working to make things better if indeed perfection is only a goal.

So many of the institutions of higher education are multipurpose institutions that usually the prospective employee can find something about the objectives of the institution with which he agrees and, if this can be extended to overall general agreement, he would have met this requirement or criterion for employment.

A qualification of less importance, but of some importance, has to do with the mores of the community and general area in which the institution is located. Most employees have families and when the employee and/or his family become very disturbed about the points of view and actions of the people who surround them, it causes them to be unhappy and often interferes with the effectiveness of their work. The whole idea is to be in a setting where it is invigorating so that it will spur the individual and the institution on to greater heights of achievement.

Physical health, mental health, and character are other qualifications needed in new personnel.

Some people act as if they are God when they interview people for jobs. They think they can look at a person and talk with him and determine whether they are in good physical and mental health and of good character. Some of these people have had to live with, or at least put up with, their misjudgments. Check the records closely and do not even rely on recommendations. Ask questions of non-references at the place or places where the candidate has worked.

Some institutions of higher learning place more emphasis on

43

character as a qualification for employment than others. Institutions that are church related claim to do so. Some, of course, do. However, some non-church-related institutions put equally as much emphasis on this point. Often character and religious affiliation become confused, but they do not need to be. Each can be dealt with objectively and without unjustified prejudice. Justified prejudice becomes acceptable when a person of a certain religious affiliation is chosen to work in an institution that is supported by that same religious affiliation after he has been judged to be the superior or equal candidate in subject matter, knowledge, and effectiveness in presenting it to students or effectiveness in applying it in research.

Choosing a person of good character regardless of his religious affiliation, if any, is very important in institutions of higher learning for the simple reason that he is dealing with students, and students so often tend to want to become like their teachers, and how a graduate acts is not only a reflection on himself but also on his institution. If a part of what is expected from graduates is to help to make the world better, it cannot be done by graduates who are not of good or high character.

Search committees with job descriptions should do their very best to get the most that they can for the money that is available. This is so very important, especially when funds are not too plentiful. With fewer personnel, all must be well-qualified and work harder.

Higher education does not have objective tests of teacher performance. It is rather ironic that in a setting where students are tested so often we do not have objective tests of the adequacy of the performance of those people who are teaching the students.

Yes, it would be a difficult undertaking. It would be somewhat similar to the situation concerning the one-time head of the Department of English at Harvard who did not have a Ph.D. and was asked why not. His reply was, "No one knows enough to test me."

Unidentified student evaluation of teachers can be helpful, but often such evaluations are seen by only the teacher. Even when "superiors," if there is such, see the student evaluations, this is not enough. Possibly someday professional societies will get around to testing by colleagues and make the results known to the individual and the administration. This would be one way in which to get the teachers to stay up-to-date in their field, the lack of which often is the reason for dissatisfaction with the teacher.

At any rate, evaluations or ratings of all employed personnel, including the head of the institution, should be made annually and kept in a cumulative record.

Some people, especially professors, may contend that formal testing or evaluation of institution employees is not necessary. They may contend that especially the faculty should be capable of self-direction. Some are and some need guidance.

Before getting into the question of what kind of information is needed, it should be stated that objective evaluation of personnel serves several purposes and all of them are of vital interest to the employees of an institution of higher learning. In the first place it causes personnel to grow--become more competent. This in turn causes the students to get better education, thus reducing or eliminating dissatisfaction. Objective evaluations give a fair basis for rank and salary promotions, thus eliminating or at least giving no credence to political or outside or inside influence based on personal favoritism. Those who officially represent the institution to the public are sometimes asked: "How do you know you are getting our money's worth out of those professors and others who are on your faculty and staff?" The representative will be able to point to the objective evaluations, thus causing the institution to get more money or backing for whatever the institution is seeking.

The lines of communication in an institution of higher learning should be kept open and used constantly. An employee can do a better job of what he is supposed to do when he has enough information to give him thorough knowledge about the institution and confidence and respect for those who are in positions of leadership.

Associates perform better when they know that their leaders have a well-founded philosophy of higher education.

Leaders of institutions of higher education have many different types of philosophies of higher education, but at least they should have one and make their decisions in keeping with it until in the light of further knowledge they see that they should amend it. Then they should do so and not try to hold to something that was not so commendable in the first place or something that has become antiquated.

For example, one type of philosophy of higher education that is based on personalism but is eclectic and pragmatic is as follows:

> Institutions of higher learning should make
> intellectual, aesthetic, and moral pursuits available to
> all secondary school graduates and adults who demonstrate
> that they can and desire to profit from a college education.
> College education should be a joint adventure of

qualified students making satisfactory progress under a qualified and conscientious faculty. Both of these groups should strive for the fullest possible development of the individual as an integral part of a meaningful society.

Higher education should be centered around the search for truth. The search for truth consists of the transmission and advancement of knowledge.

The efforts of the faculty members involve teaching, research, and service. The teaching transmits knowledge. The research is designed to advance knowledge. The service is a demonstration of the application of knowledge.

Students should be inspired and required to move along with faculty members as they teach, do their research, and render service. In doing so, the students are searching for the truth. In the process they should be taught more about how to obtain knowledge and how to evaluate it. More than that, the process should cause students to have a greater desire to acquire more knowledge and to take the initiative to obtain it. This growth in knowledge should continue not only throughout college but throughout life.

The process will reflect the teacher's personality and values. Students who like a teacher will acquire some of the teacher's personality and values.

The extracurricular program of the institution should make additional provision for personality development, acquisition of values, application of acquired knowledge in service enterprises, recreation, etc.

All institutions should require all students to meet minimum standards of the cultural heritage that is ours to transmit. This should be followed by specialization. The extent and the nature of the general and the specialized education will depend upon such factors as the qualifications of the students, the stage of advancement of humans, and the nature of any given institution of higher learning.

The objectives of the institution are printed in the institution's catalog and when these are combined with the philosophy of higher education followed by the leadership of the institution, the personnel have a good idea of what the institution as a whole is trying to accomplish and how they are going about it. The next type of information needed has to do with what is expected of each individual who is on the institution's payroll.

The duties of all personnel should be clearly stated in

writing. Job descriptions should be formulated by supervisors and those on the job. When approved by those in higher echelons who have such authority, these duties should be followed and the supervisors or those in the next higher echelon should base their annual or more frequent evaluations on such. This is especially important in regard to administrative and staff personnel. It is also necessary for teaching, research, and service personnel.

Participation and commendation are two vital factors in gaining high-quality performance of personnel.

Representation or participation in formulating policies of an institution has been, is, and increasingly will be important to employees. Of course, the board of control approves policies, many of which come from the employees to the president of the institution and then on to the board. When the board is silent on any point, the institution has the right to act. However, it is the prerogative of the board to rescind such institutional action with the adoption of a policy that is contrary.

Every institution of higher education should have a "policies manual." It is an accumulation of what is desired and how issues that have faced the institution in the past have been handled. All employed personnel of the institution and the students should be represented in making and revising such decisions. Then the administrators are charged with the responsibility of seeing that these policies are carried out. Morale of the personnel is greatly enhanced when they have a part in determining the policies. And such people will work harder to see that they are enforced.

A person is more apt to work harder when he feels that those with whom he is associated, and especially those to whom he must report or to whom he is responsible, really care for the institution and for him. Just about the best way of showing this is to keep in touch with the person's work and give him words of commendation when he does things especially well. This applies all the way from receiving a good word from someone within the institution to receiving the Nobel Prize.

It is essential to have well-qualified people employed in higher education. All people employed have an influence on the quality of the institution, and their selection should be given very careful attention. Institutions of higher learning must do more than they have in the past to improve the efficiency and effectiveness of their personnel.

Faculty

The most important group of people on the payroll of an institution of higher learning is the faculty. All other personnel at the institution, including the head of the institution, are there to do everything that they can to create conditions that will help the faculty get maximum performance out of the students. Therefore, the first priority in the expenditure of money should be on the faculty.

One of the most difficult problems in higher education is to determine the best way in which to invest money in the faculty. The difficulty is that no one really knows or will admit the real strength or weakness of a given faculty member. As mentioned earlier, there is no valid and reliable objective test of a faculty member's effectiveness. Since no one has been smart enough to come up with such, administrators have to resort to the ways of approximating effectiveness.

Tenure, rank, and salary increases are awards that are used to signify effectiveness. Any new member of a faculty must have the approval of his colleagues in his department to be recommended for tenure after three, five, seven, or whatnot years of service in a given institution. The judgment of peers in his own field of work is supposed to give the untenured faculty member a fair deal in regard to his future services at the institution. Untenured faculty members may remain employed at the institution only as long as the probation period is in effect. In a few cases, untenured faculty members may continue to teach in a given institution without tenure for a specified period of time. This is usually done when agreement cannot be reached on his tenure or there is a severe shortage of people in the field in which the person is teaching. Some prejudices come into departmental decisions about tenure. In such cases, administrators should move in and make the necessary corrections. Administrators are required to approve or disapprove all recommendations for tenure before such goes to the board of control for final approval. Some boards pay much attention to such recommendations and others merely give their stamp of approval when that line item appears in the recommended budget.

Faculty rank is determined in the same manner as described for giving tenure to faculty members. Every institution should have clearly stated minimum qualifications for each rank and this should be strictly followed.

Every promotion in faculty rank should carry with it an increase in salary in keeping with the salary schedule.

Salary schedules are very easy to determine. Take the lowest and the highest salary of each rank and then determine the mean or the median. Usually there is a great imbalance somewhere in it. Should the first allocation of funds be used to correct the imbalance? Usually it takes years to correct it along with some retirements and deaths.

A parallel question has to do with the member of faculty ranksin each department, school, or college. Are there too many or not enough associate professors, for instance, in any given department compared with the other departments throughout the institution? Should first allocations be made to correct this imbalance?

Another related question is how much money should be spent on needed new faculty members? What ranks should they be given?

An easy way out is to forget about imbalances, blaming them on stupid predecessors, and give faculty members an across-the-board raise, and then use the remaining money to attract the best faculty members that can be obtained with the money available and the reputation of the institution. Such action would not attract many, if any, outstanding new faculty members because they would then know that the present administration is stupid. Neither would it rest well with present faculty members because they want raises on the basis of merit. Of course, the merit that they prefer is their own notion of their own worth, but they will settle even after some fights and appeals on the evaluation of their peers in their own departments.

This muddled, subjective situation is ripe for takeover by unions, and they have on some campuses. Many teachers in higher education are not in favor of the unionization of faculties, but with all of the highly intellectual people assembled in institutions of higher learning there seems to be nothing on the horizon to give promise for a fair objective solution to this question. Therefore, if an answer or promising answers are not forthcoming, faculties will acquiesce to unionization with such statements as: "It's time for a change" or "What could be worse than what we have?" Administrators might think unionization will fail, and it might, but some of the smartest and well-education people of our time have been calling the shots for some of the unions. That coupled with the slogan--"Let's eliminate exploitation" would be hard to beat. The way in which to beat it is to beat them to the punch with a better system.

Some people are allergic to formulas. However, it appears that merit must be based on more than the attitude of peers. It should be based on a cluster of factors that would result in a formula that would make it possible for any given institution to adjust the value of any factor in keeping with its own philosophy, objectives, and needs.

As stated above, certainly one factor in the formula would be student evaluations of the teaching. Some teachers object to student evaluations, but such objections will subside when there is not enough money available to continue positions. Teachers,

49

however, have a point when they say that students are not mature enough to evaluate the teaching, and that time must elapse before the student sees or realizes the true value of the teaching. Some faculty members want student evaluations to be for themselves and not for anyone else. They object to even department heads seeing them much less a dean. Of course, such could be of some value to the teacher, resulting in increased effectiveness in teaching, but it would not be of value in arriving at a fair and equitable basis for giving merit raises.

Some students do not want to give teacher evaluations to which they sign their names before grades are recorded at the central recording office for fear that the evaluation might cause the teacher to lower their grades. There is some merit to this because some teachers think they are omnipotent and resent criticism, and some of them will lower the grade of such an "unappreciative jerk."

The value of a student evaluation varies with his age, the number given the class signifying the degree of difficulty of the course, who administers the evaluation, and the like. Usually one extreme will offset the other and the median will be a fairly good test of student thinking at that stage of his development.

Much more, however, is needed. Formal evaluation sheets on each teacher should be filled in by departmental chairmen every term or at least annually. These, as well as the results of the student evaluations, should be made available to the dean, and deans should check department evaluations carefully and correct any prejudices that the departmental chairmen might have in regard to any teacher.

To these two evaluations should be added the number of students taught by the teacher giving different weights to undergraduate, graduate, required or optional courses taught.

To this should be added the amount and success of authorized research done by the teacher. Again this should be based on the two evaluations and the number of students involved.

Most of the above searching for factors to be considered in the merit formula could be spurious in those cases where teachers and researchers spend most of their time trying to be popular with students, giving high grades, and courting the head of the department and the dean or even the vice-president or the president and even members of the board of control to get high ratings and/or higher salaries. Such action must be discounted by administrators.

The board's or committee's appeal must be made available within the institution for hearings for any faculty member who is of the opinion that his rating is in error.

If something of this nature can be established for merit performance, it is possible that it could carry over to the board of control as a basis for the allocation of funds to a given institution.

Salary is not the only important factor in the effectiveness of a faculty even though it is the most important. Faculty members desire and should have other things.

The closest thing to a college or university teacher, professionally speaking, other than his monthly check, is a good library. The next thing in order of importance is good students. There is no argument on either of these points. More will be stated on both of these points later.

Instructors, assistant professors, associate professors, and professors all want freedom to do their thing. This more than can be found in any other profession sets them up as a breed apart. Most of them are smart enough to know that with humans there is no such thing as absolute freedom, but often they act as though they don't know it.

A teacher wants to be "lord and master" in his classroom-- free to say or do anything he wants to do. He does not want department heads or deans or anyone else other than students who are registered in that course in his classroom to see how he is doing. He will do everything that he can to prevent such visitations. This is one of the queer things about most teachers. Really they should be honored to have visitors on occasions to see what an excellent teacher the university is privileged to have at such a low salary!

Teachers really know that they cannot do and say certain things in their classrooms and thereby their freedom is circumscribed. They know it is unprofessional to spend teaching time telling about their families or discussing their own views on anything other than the subject under consideration. They know that it is unlawful to assault a student in the classroom or anywhere else even though sometimes they feel like choking the lazy bum.

Teachers want to be protected from "witch-hunters." Witch-hunters are those people who want to get certain people fired because they are espousing something that is contrary to their own beliefs. Sometimes such is connected with the witch-hunters' desire to get the job for a relative or friend of his. Certainly administrators and boards of control should protect teachers from such attacks when what the teacher espouses is in the area of his teaching specialty. Protection in this case means backing on the basis of freedom of speech.

Faculty members would like to be free or in this case have the authority to determine the curricular offerings and requirements of the institution. This of course is the area in which the faculty is best qualified. Most colleges and universities leave such decisions or recommendations with faculty members. Often faculties of institutions are too large and unwieldy to handle such matters efficiently, and such is left to faculty senates or faculty committees. More about curricular offerings and requirements will be given later.

To have a voice in overall policy making of the institution is important to some faculty members. At one time in the distant past of higher education, faculties were in charge of and ran the entire university. Such influence has steadily declined over the years until now an estimate would be that faculties exclusively determine ten percent of the policies and they cooperate in determining another ten percent of the overall policies. Of course, such varies according to the size and type of institution. Faculty members should have a strong voice in determining policies, especially those having to do with curricular matters. This is extremely important because sometimes administrators get so involved in the mechanics of their own area of operation that they lose sight of the reason for the institution's existence which is to facilitate maximum learning.

How important is it for faculty members to counsel students? Personalized higher education is extremely important because it gets students to learn more. Counseling is the key to personalized higher education. Certainly faculty members should be expected to and they should be willing to counsel with the students who are in their classes. Here the teacher has the greatest opportunity to help the student and to help himself. It assists the student in understanding the subject matter and it kindles a desire in him to know more. This helps the teacher to get more students in his classes, not to mention the satisfaction that both he and the student feel as a result of the counseling.

Some institutions assign a certain number of students to faculty members for the planning of the student's course of study. Some of these faculty members are volunteers and others in some places are drafted to be faculty advisers. The drafted ones are usually ineffective. Often the volunteers give out misinformation. Some faculty advisers try to steer students into their own courses or into the courses offered by his department. This is done in order to survive, make a better impression, or to get higher salary raises.

Generally speaking, course-of-study advising is done better by professionally trained or educated guidance departments with the assistance of departmental heads.

To what extent should faculty members be called upon to do administrative or otherwise work at the college or university? They should be willing to help out at registration and usually they are willing to do so. They should be willing to act as faculty advisers for groups or organizations that are in or related to the faculty members' field of study, and most of them are willing to do so. Some of them are qualified and willing and do serve as faculty advisers for other groups or organizations that are in existence or should be brought into being at any given institution of higher learning.

Faculty members want excellent laboratory equipment and teaching aids. They should have such. Faculty members want the physical plant and the grounds to be of good quality, and they are especially interested in having a place to park when they come to work. Most of them have such.

The average salary in 1985 of faculty members at the colleges and universities in the USA was $31,200 plus $7,000 in fringe benefits at the public institutions and $33,000 plus $7,200 in fringe benefits at the private institutions. (Statistical abstract of the United States 1986, 106th Edition, U.S. Department of Commerce, Bureau of the Census, Washington, DC p. 157). The working conditions are helpful in getting instruction of a high quality, but the most crucial factor in having a college or university of high quality is to have a salary schedule that will hold and attract highly qualified members of the faculty.

Students

Warm bodies make up a student body. Some of them are students and some are not. All of them have met the entrance standards in one way or the other.

All of the juices of young people used to explode when they were of college age. It culminated during the sixties with international news coverage.

During the sixties they thought of practically everything to put under their umbrella of "a drive for relevance." The major emphasis of the drive was for college teachers to teach more of what is needed to perform effectively on the job after college.

A little and a lot of almost everything was under the umbrella. Students demanded that class attendance be eliminated, grades in courses be eliminated, dormitory closing hours be eliminated, open visitation by either sex in dormitory rooms be permitted at anytime, etc. In the extreme it was a demand to thrown out all rules, regulations, and standards of higher education. College and university officials had been confronted with this type of thing before, but never with so many requests with such intensity at one time. Most higher education officials failed to remember during those trying times that to encourage a pattern that responded to pressure and not to principle was to split the policy, not to nourish it.

The collegiate war went on, and the fight by young people against anyone with authority continued. They said that anyone over thirty was over the hill and therefore irrelevant. This continued under somewhat modified collegiate rules and regulations until the turbulent generations of students graduated and tried to get a job. Immediately they were confronted with the realization that those who had the jobs and controlled the dispersement of jobs were the establishment--those over thirty. For the young graduates it became a matter of changing their attitude or not having a job. The word soon trickled back to the campuses and the attitude toward the establishment become more tolerant.

For many years higher education has been trying to lure older people to enroll in non-credit or credit courses. Correspondence courses have been popular, but higher education wanted to do more. Many institutions, especially the state-supported institutions, established branch campuses throughout their states. These have become very popular. In the meantime, continuing eduction courses on the main campus have increased in enrollment. Some of these people continue their studies until they receive their first degree and others receive advanced degrees.

This desire for more education by older people has been motivated by at least two factors. One is to get a job or to get a better job or to be up-dated to hold the job. The other is that people now have more leisure time and some of them want to use some of it in a meaningful way.

At any rate, the influx of older students on the campuses has caused the composition of the student body to change and all for the better. Seemingly it has caused the younger students to be more serious about getting an education. This improves the quality of education because education is a two-way process--the thinking teacher and the thinking student.

People who work with students have to be versatile, understanding, compassionate, and firm. College students are still in the process of growing up. Some never do, but most of them make it. Growing up is very frustrating and painful. They are striving to establish their identity. Often they choose role models to try to emulate. Many of them crave attention and will do almost anything to get it. Just a little bit of attention shown them can get amazing results. Each student is somewhat different from all other students, and should be treated as such.

Hypocrisy is still the thing that students hate most in older people. They can spot it immediately and from there on that older person has no influence whatsoever with the student.

Students want to know that the people at the college care about them. This includes their peers as well as college staff members and teachers.

College students want to be known for what they are—not for what their parents have achieved or what older members of their family accomplished at that college.

College students want friends among their peers. Some of them know very little about how to make friends. Some try to be friendly and some do not. Once made, there is almost nothing that a friend will not do for his friend. This, when carried to extremes, gets some students in trouble, and sometimes that trouble is difficult for them to overcome.

To keep in shape is almost a passion among many college students. The gymnasium, the pools, the tennis courts, the track, the golf course, etc.—these are the places that are overcrowded with students. In the students' rooms in residence halls or wherever they live, they are engaged in exercising—weight lifting, etc., and then outside they go for a jog. This sort of thing has gone on in colleges for years, but now we just have more of it.

Dating comes ahead of studying for many people who are enrolled in colleges. The extent of it seems to be about the same year in and year out.

Records, tapes, and radio seem to have taken the place of television for college students. The reason seems to be that most college students do not have television sets in their rooms. They have access to television in the lobby of the dormitory or nearby, but not easy access, consequently most of them break the habit that they developed at home when they gave an inordinate amount of time to television.

Some students use drugs and alcohol and smoke a lot. Smoking has decreased among college students. Just a few are consistently on drugs. Not many drink whiskey regularly. Many students guzzle beer. One of the words used most often by some students is "six-pack."

Food services in colleges and universities generally are good and students do not use them enough. They are still on the hamburger diet and many do not eat balanced meals.

Some students enjoy bull sessions more than almost anything

else. From these much can be learned, and also much misinformation can be disseminated. Some students give too much time to them and others do not give enough.

The nonacademic problems with students seem to be mostly with the extreme introverts and the extreme extroverts. On the one hand we have the person who does too little, and on the other hand is the person who tries to do too much. Both types need help, and they have a right to get it in college. This is the job of counselors and guidance people in the institution.

Academically speaking, there are four types of undergraduates. They are (1) the beat out, (2) the conscientious worker, (3) the good student, and (4) the scholar.

Some people in this country are of the opinion that all students who receive a diploma from a secondary school have the right to enter college. Most colleges have higher admission standards, but there is some college--junior or senior--where a high school graduate can enter. Even though they have the right to enter college, many of them do not want to go to college and do not enter. Some want to enter but cannot find the money to do so even though there is much financial aid available to help them. Usually this person feels that he should earn some money immediately to help out the family. And some enter college who should not be there. These are the ones who do not want to or will not do the work that is required. These are the people who are known as the "beat outs." They should withdraw to give their places to others who are really interested in getting a college education.

The conscientious worker is the one who will set his alarm clock to get to class on time. He will use his pen and notebook to take notes as he listens to every word uttered by the professor. He has the patience to study, and takes time to study. All of these characteristics are good and they are also held by the two classifications that will be described next, but in the case of the conscientious worker, that is about all that he has to offer. Often he did not learn as much in school as he should have before he entered college. In some cases this type of person has limited mental ability. Some of these people have personal problems that are interfering with or blocking their efforts to learn. These people are the ones who almost tear the hearts out of teachers. They have personal conferences with them and really try to help them understand and remember the subject matter. Some of these students get special tutors to help them. The faculty advisers and the people in the guidance centers give much of their time to these people. Some are referred to these centers and some go for help on their own. Some are embarrassed and do not ask for assistance. Some of these people pass the course and others fail. If they do not get their personal problems straightened out or get the "hang" of how to study, they have a hard time of it and get placed on academic probation and some have to drop out of school for academic reasons.

The third type is the good student. This person is a joy to his professors. The professor states it and the student understands it. The student has prepared his assignments thoroughly. He attends class regularly. He earns a good grade, but not necessarily the highest grade.

The highest grade goes to the few--the scholars. These people do everything that is required and in addition have an inquiring mind and use it in the classroom by asking relevant questions that go beyond the assignments. They do extra work, like writing extra papers, outside the classroom. They show the professor that they have learned more about the course than he required. These are the people who often go on to graduate school.

No institution of higher learning could exist without the most essential element, and that is, students. Student effort, as guided by teachers, sets the tone and quality of the institution.

Admission and Financial Aid

There are at least two points of view in regard to admittance to college. One is that college is the privilege of all citizens and the other is that only the highly qualified academic students should be admitted.

The junior colleges have made tremendous strides in helping the senior colleges and universities solve this admissions dilemma. Much to the dismay of some senior colleges, in particular, the junior colleges have made major inroads into their enrollment because most of the junior colleges will accept any graduate of a secondary school and will accept nongraduates in certain types of vocational and technical courses. This is as it should be in a democracy.

Senior colleges and universities try to eliminate the "trial-and-error" approach to admissions and accept only those students who show promise of being able and willing to meet their graduation requirements. The prestige of the institution has much to do with the admissions requirements in that the larger the number of applicants, the higher the standards for admission become. The institution tries to get the highest qualified students it can in order to fill the number of spaces it has available.

The criteria used for admission are numerous and often arbitrary. Arbitrary in that the people at the institution do not

57

know that such criteria used for admission in fact assures the ability to meet standards to remain enrolled and meet graduation requirements. Some of the criteria used are College Board Examination scores, scores on tests provided by the American Colleges Testing Program, rank in high school, high school scholastic average, intelligence test scores, participation in high school activities, athletic ability, children of alumni, wealth of parents, character, health, etc.

A college or university has the right to survive and even flourish if able, and willing students have the opportunity to receive a higher education. This does not mean that every student who finishes secondary school can enter the college of his choice regardless of what kind of scholastic record he made in high school, how much mental ability he has, or how much money he has or can get to pay for or help pay for his college education. But it does mean that he should at least be able to try his hand at a junior college or at an off-campus center of a university if he received his high school diploma, even if he does not have or if his family does not have the money to pay for it. County, state, and federal financial assistance to the institution pays for a part of such, and scholarships and loans should take care of the rest of it.

A large amount of money is available to give financial assistance to students in colleges and universities. It comes from the county, district, state, federal government, private citizens who have given to the foundation of a college or university or who have established scholarships directly to the college or university, businesses, industry, labor unions, etc.

The amount for 1985-86 was twenty-one billion. Forty-seven percent of the money was for grants, fifty percent for loans, and three percent for part-time work. (Trends in Student Aid: 1980 to 1986, College Board Publications, New York, NY, 1986).

It appears that from all of this money anyone could get a scholarship or a loan. However, it does not always work out that way. Every scholarship or loan has been established for a specific purpose and either the donor or the institution of higher learning or both have set up the requirement that must be met in order to obtain the money. Some institutions of higher learning have turned down gifts for loans and/or scholarships because the donor wanted to set up criteria that were not in keeping with the purpose of the college or university. Such is rare.

Information concerning loans and scholarships and the requirements for such may be obtained from the admissions officer or director of financial aid at the institution of the individual's choice, and it should be obtained well in advance of the desired entry date.

Much more research needs to be done on aptitudes for college education. If a scholarship or loan is based exclusively on financial need, that within itself is easy to determine and easy for the prospective student and his parents and friends to understand. However, if all or a part of the financial aid is based on a student's attributes to make good scholastically in college, that is a different matter. At this point very little is known and some college and university officials take the line of least resistance by adopting something as an expediency measure in getting the job done, giving little or no thought to how such can be an injustice to the applicant. For instance, scores on College Board Examinations have a very low correlation with grades earned in college, yet some colleges and universities exclude all students who score below a certain figure on the College Board Scholastic Aptitude Test. A score on only one test is not necessarily a correct assessment of a person's ability to successfully complete the requirements for a degree. Admission to college should be made on the basis of a combination of factors. Admission officers can and should do better.

The way in which to get the job done in keeping with the best that is known is for someone at the college or university to work out a regression equation that will have the highest possible correlation between the sum of the factors employed in the formula and grade-point averages during the first term, the first year, the lower division, and the four-year span.

Items chosen for the equation should come from the factors that are associated with college success. It is known that students who do well on the following factors make good grades in college: intelligence tests, nonstandardized examinations, high school grades, rank in secondary school graduating class, certain personal characteristics such as industry, reliability, attitude, perseverance, ambition, purposefulness, capacity for study; and students from good social and environmental backgrounds.

In all fairness to any prospective student, it must be said that predictions of success in college are more appropriate for groups than for individuals. Consequently, an institution can know more accurately how many members of the freshman class will be eligible, from a scholastic point of view, to return for the sophomore year. And in most cases, the prediction for individuals that are made on the basis of a regression equation are very apt to be accurate. But any individual college student can change his own prediction and get a higher grade-point average if he has sufficient mental ability and if he has learned the basics in high school. From there on if the student does not have too many personal problems bothering him and if his health does not both him and if he really applies himself by studying hard every day and--more than anything else--if he really wants to make good, he can make it. These are the people who give college and university teachers and administrators a thrill. And many of them use the same habits that they developed in college in their line of work after college and turn out to be some of the most responsible and successful people in the community.

All colleges and universities recruit students at one time or the other. The reasons for recruiting are numerous. Colleges and universities prefer not to recruit because it is time-consuming and expensive. Also to recruit is a little bit embarrassing. It is to admit that the program of the institution is not effective enough to draw the size and kind of student body that is desired. In other words, there is a compulsion behind recruiting. Possibly more students are needed in order to have enough money to make the budget balance. Many institutions state that they recruit for better students. They would like for the entering class each year to have a high average on the Scholastic Aptitude Test or on some other test. Some institutions prefer to have students from all sections of the nation and they recruit in order to obtain better geographical representation. This gives students a wider range of experiences to fit them better for employment and living anywhere in the country. Also it gives the institution more of a national reputation.

The same reasoning applies to recruiting students from other countries. This is considered by some people of great importance because the more that people get to know each other, the better they understand each other and soon they find they have more in common than they have differences. This promotes peace. Also, some foreigners who are educated in this country and who return to their native lands improve the condition of their countries, which makes a better world. Foreign students can give an institution an intellectual boost. They give natives more competition thus raising the quality of learning in the institution.

Laws and federal regulations call for no discrimination of any kind in the admission of students other than on their scholastic ability and achievements. This has caused many institutions to recruit blacks and students from other minority groups.

Recruitment of athletes is about as well known as any type of recruitment. It will be discussed briefly in the section of this book entitled "Intercollegiate Athletics." This type o   f recruiting is more intense than any other in higher education.

Recruitment of outstanding scholars to do graduate work is done by practically every institution of higher learning that offers graduate work. It takes brains, knowledge, and dedication to do outstanding graduate work, and graduate and professional schools compete fiercely for such. So do students who want the graduate fellowships and entrance into the more prestigious schools. With such students, the post-baccalaureate programs have a better chance of pushing back the boundaries of knowledge, which is the top objective of research work.

Recruitment is selling. Salesmanship is a field all of its own, but in higher education it depends upon a number of items.

The quality of the program at the institution is the most effective item in recruiting. This refers primarily to what a person gets in the process of qualifying for the degree. Effective teaching at the institution is the most important tool in the recruiter's kit.

The second most important item in the recruiter's kit is financial aid. Practically every prospective students want some type of financial aid. Many students want it because they know that they cannot go to college without it. Their families do not have enough money to finance it, and they themselves have not been able or think they will not be able to make enough money to finance it. Some other prospective students who can get or have enough money to finance it want a scholarship to justify or recognize their hard work and scholastic achievement in secondary school. Some want it merely to satisfy their ego, and if they get a scholarship, they brag about it and even flaunt it in the faces of some of their peers. A few institutions award scholarships to students whose parents make enormous salaries or have large annual incomes. The reasoning behind this is that such people have lifestyles that require all that they earn or take in, and this type of living will not change, and if the offspring does not get a scholarship, he or she cannot enter college. Giving scholarships to such students is questionable in the minds of some people, but justifiable to the institutions when such graduates make good records and make large contributions to the endowment.

People like to be connected with a winning team. If the institution has a winning intercollegiate football team or is outstanding in some other athletic endeavor, it does not hurt the recruiter one bit. It is helpful, but not essential.

Of course, there are many other reasons why a prospective student chooses to apply for admission to any given institution, and it is the business of the admissions office to know them and tailor the institution's presentations in keeping with them.

An essential in recruiting is to have an attractive catalog and very attractive brochures to give to prospective students. This is discussed in the section of this book entitled "Public Relations."

There are many ways of getting the information to the

prospective students. Basically these are through the media, in the mail, and in person.

Some institutions at a given time are not interested in increasing the size of the student body, and in some instances some people in the institution are interested in increasing enrollment and others are not. In the cosmopolitan city where this section is being written, it has been reported that the president of the undergraduate student council is writing letters to high school guidance counselors asking them not to suggest the University of Miami as a college choice. Staff members of the same university are working to increase the size of the student body in order to have that additional money to raise faculty salaries thereby offsetting inflation and retaining effective faculty members and attracting others.

Other institutions, and these are few in number, are interested in decreasing the size of the student body. This is usually desired by the alumni/ae or some board members and not by the administration, teachers, and students. Such is easy to do. Cut out recruiting and raise the standards for admission. This will achieve the end in practically no time.

The College Blue Book, published by the MacMillan Publishing Co., Inc., in New York City, is a reference book in libraries that provides narrative descriptions of colleges and universities; the degrees offered by college and subject; and scholarships, fellowships, grants, and loans offered by colleges and universities. This information is in three separate volumes. The volume on financial aid lists such according to area studies: environmental studies, humanities, life sciences, medical sciences, minorities, physical sciences, social sciences, and technology.

Paperbacks are available in most libraries and bookstores on how to prepare to pass examinations for entrance to college. They carry such titles as How to Pass National Merit Scholarship Tests, Preparing to Take the Scholastic Aptitude Test, American College Testing Program Examinations, Graduate Record Examination Preparation, etc.

An essential is for colleges and universities to get more reliable and valid methods of determining which students should be accepted.

In the meantime, the competition for students among the colleges and universities will continue. Some of the institutions will accept warm bodies and others will accept the brightest, most knowledgeable, and most earnest students. And most of the institutions will claim that their admission standards were and are such as to enhance the quality of higher education.

Chapter 5

PROGRAM

This chapter has sections on curricula, standards, teaching, research, and public service.

Curricula--Undergraduate and Graduate

What do you have to offer? That is one of the most intriguing questions in existence. The crux of the answer to this question, as far as higher education is concerned, is the curricula.

Of course, every institution of higher learning has more to offer than the curricula. They have outstanding professors, beautiful campuses, high-caliber students, winning athletic teams, personalized attention, prestige, etc.

Every institution offers instruction. Most of them offer opportunities for research. Some of them offer public service. However, all of them offer diplomas or degrees. The diplomas have to do with specialties of less than baccalaureate-level work and usually come from junior colleges.

Junior or community colleges offer the vocational and technical courses for students who plan to go on the job immediately after they complete the course of study, and they offer courses of study that lead to the last two years of work in a senior college. Some junior colleges offer only the transfer to senior college curricula. However, typical offerings in these institutions are as follows:

PROGRAMS OF STUDY
BUSINESS TECHNOLOGY
   Accounting
   Commercial Graphics
   Computer Programming
   General Business
   Industrial Management Technology
   Management
   Marketing
   Secretarial Science
   General Office
   Clerk-Typist
   Microcomputer Business Applications
   Microcomputer Programming
   Word Processing
   Word Processing for Secretaries

HEALTH SCIENCES TECHNOLOGY

Dental Laboratory Technology
Medical Laboratory Technology
Nursing (ADN)
Nursing (ADN) Advanced Track
Radiologic Technology
Respiratory Therapy
Horticultural Technology
Dental Assisting
Hospital Pharmacy Technician

INDUSTRIAL AND ENGINEERING TECHNOLOGY

Aircraft Maintenance Technology
Chemical Engineering Technology
Civil Engineering Technology
Electrical Engineering Technology
Electronics Engineering Technology
Machine Tool Technology
Mechanical Engineering Technology
Vocational-Technical Education
Air Conditioning/Refrigeration Mechanics
Automotive Mechanics
Diesel Equipment Mechanics
Industrial Drafting
Industrial Electricity/Electronics
Industrial Mechanics
Machine Tool
Welding
Construction Drafting
Advanced Construction Drafting
Construction Management
Advanced Construction Management
Surveying
Advanced Surveying

RELATED STUDIES

Associate in Arts
Associate in Science

Over the years in this country the number of required courses in a curriculum at the senior college level has varied from all to practically not any. The elective system as originated at Harvard gave students a wide range of choice of courses. This system was carried so far that during the sixties students in some institutions could choose almost all of his courses. Since then the trend has been in the opposite direction. Usually, however, there is a core curriculum that is required of all students. In a senior college, this consists of requirements in English, history, and science. Sometimes courses in mathematics and foreign languages are included. The general idea is to catch up on any deficiencies that the student might have experienced in high school and raise the student's level of proficiency in the humanities, natural sciences, physical sciences, and in social studies, with the greatest amount of emphasis being placed on proficiency in English because this is the language that most of the students in this country will use to convey his needs, wishes, and his knowledge.

After meeting the requirements of the core curriculum, the student who is working for his bachelor's degree has to meet a concentration requirement. This requires him to satisfactorily complete a certain number of courses in the subject in which he chooses to major. Just as the core curriculum requires almost two years of work (four semesters), so does the requirement of concentration require approximately two years of work. In some majors there are fewer opportunities for choice of courses than in others. For instance, in home economics and in civil engineering, more specialized courses are specified than for those who major in say English or history.

The goals and purposes of the institution come into the degree requirements of some institutions, especially the institutions that are church-related. Here the study of Bible is required for a degree. Sometimes other courses in religion and philosophy are required.

As students move on after receiving a bachelor's degree to graduate or professional school, the courses required become more specialized. Students in graduate schools working for master's degrees have a bit of latitude for choosing courses within majors, but for practically all other degrees the courses are specified and required. The idea here is that those who formed the curriculum know, or think they know, what a student has to know in order to be successful in that given field of work.

The Master's degree program usually consists of one year of course work beyond the Bachelor's degree, a thesis, and a comprehensive examination. Some institutions require the student to pass an English Proficiency examination. Some institutions require two years of work for the Master's degree.

The Doctor of Philosophy degree is offered in many fields of study. Students who seek this degree must pass a written or an oral examination and in some cases both a written and an oral examination at least one year before the degree is to be granted. In some cases, this admission to candidacy examination is given immediately after the student receives a Master's degree. After passing this examination a student must satisfy a residence requirement which usually is three years in an approved university and at least one year of this work must be in the university from which the degree is to be received. In most cases a foreign language requirement must be met. This can be in English for foreign students. Some universities permit computer science or statistics to be substituted for a foreign language. A comprehensive examination is required and it must be both written and oral in the field in which the student is working. Usually this is required at least sixty days before the degree is to be granted. No later than five years after the candidate has taken his comprehensive examination he must present a dissertation based on his research and he must defend it successfully no later than thirty days before he expects to receive the degree.

In addition to Junior College curricula, baccalaureate curricula in senior colleges and universities, Masters degrees and doctorates in graduate schools, higher education also offers professional education, cooperative education, interinstitutional education, extension education, correspondence education, military education, agriculture education, and religious education.

Using professional education as an example, first professional degrees are offered in dentistry, medicine, optometry, osteopathic medicine, choropastic, law, theology and several others in which only a few students are enrolled.

Then taking only one medical school as an illustration degrees and certificates are offered in thirty-nine programs as follows:

COLLEGE OF ALLIED HEALTH SCIENCES
Master in Health Sciences
Bachelor of Science
   -Cytotechnology
   -Dental Hygiene
   -Extracoporeal Circulation Technology
   -Medical Record Administration
   -Medical Technology
   -Occupational Therapy
   -Physical Therapy
   -Radiologic Technology
   -Respiratory Therapy
Advanced Certificates
   -Anesthesia for Nurses
   -Orthoptic/Ophthalmic Technology
Associate Degree
   -Dental Laboratory Technology
   -Histotechnology
   -Medical Laboratory Technology
   -Nursing
   -Radiologic Technology
   -Respiratory Therapy

Certificates
  -Dental Assisting
  -Histologic Technique
  -Hospital Pharmacy Technician
  -Practical Nursing

COLLEGE OF DENTAL MEDICINE
Doctor of Dental Medicine

COLLEGE OF GRADUATE STUDIES
Master of Science & Doctor of Philosophy
  -Anatomy
  -Biochemistry
  -Biometry
  -Pathology
  -Physiology
  -Basic and Clinical Immunology & Microbiology
  -Pharmacology
Doctor of Philosophy
  -Molecular & Cellular Biology & Pathobiology
  -Pharmaceutical Sciences

COLLEGE OF MEDICINE & COLLEGE OF GRADUATE STUDIES
Doctor of Medicine-Doctor of Philosophy

COLLEGE OF MEDICINE
Doctor of Medicine

COLLEGE OF NURSING
Master of Science in Nursing
Bachelor of Science in Nursing
Certificate in Nursing Midwifery

COLLEGE OF PHARMACY
Doctor of Pharmacy
Bachelor of Science in Pharmacy

According to the 1986 Statistical Abstract of the United States, U.S. Department of Commerce, Bureau of the Census, the most recent figures on the number of degrees offered a year was as follows: 560,700 less than Bachelor's Degree, 969,504 Bachelor's Degree, 289,921 Master's Degree, 33,088 Doctor's, 15,484 Medicine, 5,585 Dentistry, 36,540 Law, 111,451 Engineering, etc.

More and more people have been and are enrolling in Continuing Education courses. These are people who have never been to college, those who had their college education interrupted, and those who have a degree and would like to continue their education to hold their jobs or to qualify for promotions, or to simply enjoy learning more. Some of these courses are non-credit and others are for credit.

Some of the non-credit courses at an average size senior college are as follows: Communication Skills for Managers, Fundamentals of Finance and Accounting for Non-Financial Managers, Leadership Skills, How to Build Memory Skills, How to Win at Office Politics and Still be an Effective Leader, Dynamics of Employee Motivation, Speak for Yourself, Audio-Visual Presentations, Your Professional Impact, Introduction to the IBM PC, Lotus 1-2-3, dBase III, dBase III Advanced, Optional IBM PC Computer Courses, Great Decisions '86, Psychology of Intimacy for Professionals, Marriage and Family Therapy, Grants Workshop, Office Management for Professionals, Wines of the World, Newsletter Layout and Design, Psychology of Intimacy, Rhythmic Aerobics, Analysis of Income Real Estate, Financing of Real Estate, Writing for Fun and Profit, Interior Design, and Basic 35mm Photography.

The courses for credit offered by Continuing Education Centers of colleges and universities are for undergraduate and graduate credit. They are regular courses that are offered by the institution. An undergraduate degree is required to take graduate courses. A continuing education student does not have to meet admission standards in order to audit or take for credit an undergraduate course. Special permission from the instructor is required in this institution for the student to audit a course. Courses for continuing education students are available only on a space available basis. Under state law this state supported institution offers all continuing education courses to senior citizens who are sixty years of age or older without charge.

The above leads up to several questions that are vitally important for the future of higher education and for the future of our nation and the world. It has to do with curriculum construction. What constitutes an educated person? When is a person adequately educated or trained to begin work in a profession or in other types of work? Who makes these determinations? How often are they made? Who should make them and how should they go about making such important decisions and how often should they do so?

Historically, these decisions have been made by faculties based on what they considered to be important and, generally speaking, they would make these determinations as seldom as possible. Many colleges and universities have merely imitated or duplicated curricular requirements from more prestigious institutions, especially those that were the first or among the first to be established in this country.

An enormous number of courses have been added in catalog offerings by new professors who have such as their specialties. Much of this has been for the good in that it caused the curricular offerings to be more relevant.

Much has been written from the beginning of recorded history on what constitutes an educated person. Some faculty members or administrators in every institution should have had thorough instruction along those lines and should be able and willing to feed such past history into the contemporary hopper.

Curriculum committees and faculty senates have recommended and approved changes in curricular requirements over the years. Such is the prerogative of the faculty subject to administrative approval and in case of new degrees, such goes to the board of control for approval.

What does it take to get a curriculum changed or reevaluated? Does it take pressure from a state, regional, or professional accrediting group to get action? In some instances that is the way it is done. Does it take action by the board of control to get such a study done? Usually boards do not call for such. Does it take action from the president of the institution to get such a reevaluation done? Usually they do not call for such, leaving well enough along and giving their time where the pressure is the greatest. Does the request come from the students? Usually not because they do not consider themselves expert enough to call for such and usually they do not realize how much they did not learn in college until they get out on the job. The major exception to this was the student call for relevance during the sixties. Do faculty members call for reevaluation of curricular requirements? Usually not. Generally they are content to let well enough along. However, there are those faculty members who are teaching courses that are not required for graduation and they want them to be required. However, these faculty members are met by other faculty members who have vested interests in their courses that are required and they do not want such changed.

The desire by some or many faculty members for the courses that they teach to be required is based on self-interest. It is somewhat like tenure. Some teachers are so very confident about the quality of their teaching that they do not care whether their courses are required or whether they have tenure. They know that their good teaching will draw students to their classes and they will have a job just as long as such is the case. Of course, tenure is more involved. It protects the teacher against personal animosity and arbitrary administration. On the other hand, sometimes tenure insures poor teaching.

There is not a scientific approach to curriculum construction. It is a philosophical approach. It should remain a philosophical procedure, and not be replaced by, but aided by, computer technology and techniques from business.

Curriculum reevaluation in higher education is badly in need of some guidelines.

The first guideline should be that every college and university should reevaluate all of its curricular requirements for all diplomas and degrees at least every four years. This includes the courses required, the amount of credits required, the grade average required, and all else that is required for a diploma or a degree.

Secondly, in order to give students protection against many possible changes, all students should be assured in the catalog that they will get their degrees based on the catalog statements of the year in which they started their college work at that institution if they complete it within seven years. If not completed within seven years, the catalog for the eighth year will be followed for the succeeding seven years and so on. This becomes increasingly important as more older people take courses in colleges and universities. Many of these people do not plan to meet degree requirements, but sometimes they change their minds about it and of course they have the right to do so but their degrees should be updated by the rule or policy as stated above.

Thirdly, reevaluation committees could be composed of mostly faculty members, a few administrators, a few students, and a few alumni. This committee could have the assistance of the institution's Department of Institutional Research to provide data and do much detailed work. There could be one committee for undergraduate work, another for graduate work, and one for each of the professional schools connected with the institution. Each committee should report its work to its own faculty and faculty action should be passed on to the administration for the recommendation of the deans and vice-presidents and the approval of the president. All new programs for degrees should be presented by the president to the board of control for approval.

Fourthly and most importantly, these committees should get all of the facts that they can and use all of the vision that they can muster to determine what the students will need in order to cope with what will face them during their lifetime, but at least for the next ten years, and then come back for updating—continuing education. In other words, shoot for fifty years but settle if necessary for ten.

The goals of the institution must be considered by the committees. If these goals are relevant then the requirements should reflect it. If they are not relevant, the committees should say so and make recommendations to change them in such a way as to make them relevant. These recommended changes must go through established channels.

One rather vexing present-day problem is that present-day students, according to test scores, are not as well-qualified for college work as students have been in the immediate past.

Certainly the starting point for the curriculum reevaluation committees is to consider the qualifications of the students who are admitted to the college.

Proliferation is the best way in which to describe the number of courses listed in college and university catalogs. One way in which to reduce the cost of operating an institution of higher learning is to cut the number of courses offered, thus requiring fewer faculty members. It appears that senior colleges and universities will have to do this if they admit fewer students. This will not necessarily be harmful. It could and should cause the remaining courses to have more content and be more relevant.

Another way in which institutions or board of control will save money in the future is to eliminate duplication of courses between institutions within commuting distances of each other. This is difficult to do because each institution usually wants to hold onto what it has, but with financial pressure becoming more intense, they will be more likely to yield on this point.

Of course, curricular offerings are essential in colleges and universities, but it is imperative that duplication and prolification in such offerings be eliminated.

Curricular changes have taken place constantly since they were first installed at the first colleges to be established in this country. Curricula committees recommend changes to faculty senates and those that are approved are sent on to the administration for approval. They are put into operation after the president of the institution approves them. Usually only new degree offerings and degree deletions are acted upon by the Board of Control.

The typical institution now makes some curricular changes each year. All of this is quality control because the changes are designed to make the offerings and requirements more relevant and effective.

Teaching

Trial, error, success, or failure--that almost describes teaching at the college and university level. However, in order to have the opportunity to do this, a person must have a certain number of degrees or certain accomplishments in his field of specialization. An artist, for instance, without a degree could be on the faculty of a college. Some people with only baccalaureate degrees are on faculties of some colleges--especially junior colleges. Usually, though, a person must have a master's degree or a doctorate to have the opportunity to teach in a college or university in this country.

There is no certification of college or university teachers as we have of teachers at the elementary and secondary levels. Some of these teachers have had courses in how to teach while they were in college, but most of them have not. Some of them held teaching assistantships or fellowships when they were in the process of getting their advanced degrees. Some of these were closely supervised by experienced professors and some were not.

In colleges and universities it is assumed that if a person knows something he can effectively transmit it to his students. This is not necessarily the case, and why intelligent people in higher eduction think so is a mystery that has not been solved. There is really no adequate defense of it. Nevertheless, teaching is exciting.

The thrill that is experienced more often in higher education comes when a "spark" ignites between teacher and student. Reference here is not being made to the "crush" that a few students have for their teachers or a few teachers have for their students. There have been some affairs between students and teachers, some of which have wrecked the lives of some people involved and some that resulted in marriage. Some of them have gotten married without the aid of affairs. Teachers must be aware at all times that most students are younger and are in the process of "trying their wings" and often want to see how far they can go not thinking about the consequences. It is the job of the teacher to keep the student-teacher relationship professional at all times. Of course, anyone can make a charge that someone made an advance toward him or her. In colleges and universities charges are made by both sexes on both sides—students and teachers. However, not many charges are filed. Administrators do not tolerate anyone making advances toward anyone. Usually the charges come from students about teachers. When such are received, administrators usually call together a committee of the teacher's peers to hear the case, and then the administration takes action on the findings. Guilty teachers are usually suspended or dismissed. Sometimes such charges go beyond the hearings and action on the campus. At times teachers employ attorneys and the cases are heard and settled in court. College and university administrators should not take these cases lightly because the teacher's professional career and even his family life could depend upon the outcome.

Now back to the thrill. The thrill comes when learning takes place. Why should this be a thrill? Isn't it what education is all about? Shouldn't it take place all the time? The answer to the last question is that it doesn't. But when it does, it makes the student happy and it also makes the teacher happy. Learning can work both ways. Once in awhile a student says something that teaches the teacher something. This could be called a super thrill. Many students think they know more than their teachers, and in some cases this is true. For instance, in painting or in piano a student could perform better than the teacher. In such instances, the teacher teaches the student to become even more proficient.

There is no one accepted method of teaching in institutions of higher learning. Each teacher has his own way of doing it, and also it varies according to subject matter.

Teachers work hard to figure out the best way in which they can get the greatest amount of the subject matter that they are teaching across to the greatest number of students. One reason why this is so very difficult is because the students vary so much in their educational backgrounds and in their interests. Theoretically, every teacher should know the educational background of every student, but this is seldom known except in exceedingly small classes when the teacher takes the initiative to find out or when the teacher has a personal conference with a student for the purpose of ascertaining this information. One reason why some students are of the opinion that their college teachers are not personally interested in them is because they feel that some teachers do not want to take the time to have counseling conferences with them and they do not make the effort to ask for a conference.

Many college teachers use the lecture method of teaching. Here they talk about the subject from the time the class begins and continue to do so until it ends. Students are supposed to take notes as the lecture proceeds. Some do and some do not. Often in such classes only one examination is given at the end of the term and the grade that a student makes on the examination is the grade that he receives for the course. The teacher has the right to handle his course in this manner unless there is some regulation within the institution stating otherwise. The writer has had a policy in the institutions where he has served as academic dean and president that all teachers must base a term grade on more than one indicator, and a clear record should be kept by the teacher of each student's performances. The reason for the first part of this policy is simple justice, and the reason for the latter part is to have something concrete to settle complaints and in a few cases lawsuits. Any given student might be ill at the time of a final examination or he might be mentally disturbed at that time and he might request another examination. It is not wise to give more than one final examination because it is difficult, if not impossible, to make the two examinations equal in difficulty. But when the teacher gives several tests during the term and lets it be known that the tests count so much and the final examination counts so much, there can be little argument about the final grade unless the teacher made a mistake in calculations, in which instance, he embarrassingly makes the correction.

Most college teachers use the modified lecture method of teaching. Here the teacher will give the students a mimeographed outline of the aspects of the subject that will be given consideration during the term. Usually this outline will be accompanied by a list of books and periodicals that deal with the areas that will be considered during the course. The students are encouraged to go to the library and read some of the references that are being discussed because the teacher will ask them about such writings. Sometimes the teacher will require each student to write a paper of approximately a certain length about any of the topics on the outline that they choose and turn it in prior to the end of the course. The teacher will state that a part of the final grade will be based on the quality of the paper presented. Then the teacher will introduce the first topic on the outline by lecturing on it. After doing so he will call for discussion. Usually this is done by calling on individuals to answer certain questions as posed by the teacher. Often the teacher will ask students to elaborate on the topic from what he has read in the library. Lively discussions often take place and here is where most of the sparks fly and most of the thrills are experienced.

Some courses, such as biology and chemistry, have laboratory work connected with the theory part of the course. The students learn the theory during the lecture-discussion sessions, and learn even more when they do a little testing and experimenting in the laboratory sessions. One of the best ways of learning is by doing under expert supervision.

Some of the more advanced courses are taught by the seminar method. Here fewer students are in the course, and more discussion takes place. Usually these courses demand more out-of-class work. Some of them have field trips to observe what they are learning in action.

Usually more learning takes place in small classes. Higher education has been remiss, as a whole, in permitting classes to get too large, especially at the lower division level. This has caused more teachers to resort to the lecture method where less learning usually takes place. Although many teachers have tried to offset this situation by using every conceivable mechanized instrument to appeal to the various senses.

Telecommunication technologies are permeating higher education. Institutions are offering television-based courses available through Public Broadcasting Service. Audio-based courses are finding an increasing number of users among colleges and universities. They can be broadcast on radio, played in the classroom, or used at any location where students have access to audio cassette equipment. By using computer mail and computer conferencing systems student interaction can be achieved. A few universities are working to provide complete telecommunications capabilities to all faculty and students. Learning stations connecting faculty and students and with databases and computational programs are being placed in libraries, dormitories, classrooms, and laboratories. More and more faculty members are now writing programs for the computers. This software has been hard to come by, but some now predict a computer revolution in higher education as a result of professors apparent willingness to move into writing what to put on the software to more effectively teach the course.

There should be a requirement of accrediting associations that all beginning teachers in colleges and universities be given supervision on a regular basis for a period of a year by an experienced teacher within the department in which he is teaching.

More than that, the accrediting association should require the head of every department to give a rating of effectiveness in teaching and the extent the teacher is keeping up in his field at the end of each term, and such evaluations should be filed in the office of the dean of the college in which the person is teaching. Such evaluations should be available to the teacher himself and to the vice-president and president of the institution.

Workload is a problem among teachers. Full-time faculty members teach approximately twelve class hours of approximately fifty minutes each per week. This number of class hours varies with the type of classes being taught. Naturally more hours can be taught by any given teacher at the lower division level than at the doctoral level. To the layman this small number of hours for teachers to work in the classroom seems to be an unusually light load. However, some studies have indicated that approximately one-third of college and university teachers suffer from job stress. This stress results in anxiety, depression, and insomnia. They say it comes from not having enough time to do professional reading, lack of class-preparation time, too much committee work, red tape, and finances.

Good teaching is associated with good health, and every precaution should be taken by administrators not to overwork those who are doing the teaching and the research work.

Some institutions of higher learning select a "Teacher of the Year" to motivate excellent teaching. Most good teachers do not need such motivation, but all teachers, like other humans, like to have their work appreciated.

Nothing is more essential to a college or university than good and excellent teaching because this is the prime function of the institution and here is where most of the quality of the institution is generated.

What controls are there on teachers to see that they are doing a good job of teaching? Some people are of the opinion that a tenured full professor comes on close to having absolute freedom when he is in his classroom as anyone else anywhere at anytime. That could be correct, but still he has some constraints if not controls on him. He wants to have students to teach. Very few courses are required and if so usually more than one teacher teaches them. The professor needs to do well enough in the classroom for students to choose to take his course. Even tenured full professors usually want to have the respect of his colleagues at least those in the department in which he is teaching. His colleagues form opinions of their fellow department members from what the professor says to them and what the students say about the professor. In a few rare cases department members visit each other's classes. Usually the professor wants the department head, the academic vice-president and the president to think well of his work especially when it comes time to make determinations in regard to salary raises. Some institutions give objective tests in some subjects and the performance of the students under a given teacher can be compared with the performance of students in the same subject under other teachers in that institution and in other institutions. A few institutions have student ratings of teachers and some teachers think they are of little value but still they could be a restraint on some teachers.

The most important quality control within an institution of higher learning is the testing of students. The student who earns a bachelor's degree must earn approximately one hundred and thirty semester hours of credit and in the process he has approximately thirty teachers during those four years of work. These thirty teachers test a given student approximately five hundred times during the time that he takes to complete the one hundred and thirty semester hours of work. And in graduate work the testing is approximately half as often. This testing takes the form of teacher asking a given student a question in class and recording the student's answer in his grade-book, written tests, termpapers, objective written tests, results of laboratory experiments, and final examinations.

The student who gets his degree knows that he has been thoroughly tested by many people, and it is his hope that the standards used by his teachers were high enough to assure him an education of high quality. A documentation of this hope is what is being called for at this time.

Some people, especially those at state governmental levels, are calling on higher education for assessment at the undergraduate level. By this most of them mean that they want higher education to develop some measurable way in which to test undergraduates just before they receive the bachelor's degree. It is an instrument of accountability.

Many people are obsessed with numbers and they want a number attached to the above assessment. This can be done by asking professors to revert from the alphabetical to the numerical method of grading. This method can be used in the comprehensive examinations for baccalaureate candidates. These comprehensives could be weighted for results on general studies, majors, minors, English proficiency and any other important parts of the examination. The undergraduate exit score could the average of what is given the student by the examining professors.

This score could be the retention index of how much of what he has learned he can repeat or write without the aids of books, etc. Such is important for quick decisions, but most of life is an open-book examination.

One would have to expect these undergraduate exit examination scores to vary within a department, within a school, and within a college or university. Such scores within one institution of higher learning would vary with the scores in another such institution.

Possibly a new organization to be called the Council on USA Higher Education could be formed to establish guidelines that would get the scores to be more comparable. Such a Council should be composed of educators and not politicians from the state or federal level.

All of this might satisfy politicians but it should be remembered that politicians must have something to talk about and they look for a handle to catch and they select the one that they think will get them the most votes. Nevertheless, some of them are sincerely interested in improving higher education and they should receive all the support that they can be given.

The undergraduate exit score could motivate students to study harder and try to retain what they have learned longer. Such would be a definite improvement, although some colleges now have undergraduate comprehensive examinations.

The Graduate Record Examination has been in existence for sometime. The writer was the first person to administer it. It is helpful in assessing the suitability of students to enter graduate work, but it would not be a true test of what the undergraduate was supposed to learn for a degree in say civil engineering or home economics. Most of the students who receive such an education do not go into graduate work. They get a job and the quality of their education is the major interest of the people who are calling for assessment.

The Exit Score procedure could be used not only for the bachelor degree graduates, but also for all graduates who are granted graduate degrees. This would not be very different from the comprehensive examinations that are now being given for advanced degrees. These Exit Scores for specific degrees granted will be a test of effectiveness in teaching and learning.

To test the relevance of what a student is taught a Performance Score could be obtained by the college or university from employers of each graduate to give the graduate a score from one hundred to five hundred, or some other numerical range, once a year for five, ten, or whatever length of time desired. The average of these ratings would be the individual's Performance Score at any given time. Ratings for self-employed graduates could be the average score from three of his or her competitors. For those few who are unemployed or who have enough wealth and choose not to be employed the record should show such a condition.

Of course, this Performance Score rates a person in only one aspect of his or her life. Other ratings could be obtained in family life, community leadership, etc.

Research

Every faculty member is interested in research. All of them do some kind of research work, if nothing more than reading their professional journals. Members of the faculty who are scholars are vitally interested in research. They want to learn as much as can be learned about their specialization and publish what their research has uncovered. Most scholars would like to break the barriers that divide the known from the unknown in their field and even win the Nobel Prize.

Organized university research is supported from university funds, and funds from state agencies, federal government, foundations, scholarly and professional societies, individual donors, and business and industry.

Grants and contract payments are made to the university, and in turn go to mature students as fellowships or grants-in-aid, and to faculty members as salaries and/or grants.

There is no known limit to what the human mind can do, and research is where only limited equipment can halt the progress. Vast amounts of equipment are needed for some experimental research and usually it is very costly. Some are so very costly that they are not being assembled on the university campus. Instead, industry is taking the research professor from the university and having him do research work at the plant.

In recent years, developments in computer technology have been a boom to research. Through data processing so very much of the laborious mathematical and processing work has been eliminated

78

leaving the researcher more time to think and dive deeper into his inquiry.

There are two other kinds of research. One kind is called sponsored research. This is the type that is entirely financed by the person outside of the university or the firm that has a problem and would like for the experts at the university to research it and solve it. For instance, a dry cleaning firm could have some trouble with losing the color in certain types of garments and would want the university to find out what they can do to correct the problem. The textile and clothing department of the university could be interested and accept the request. If these people can solve the problem, the people at the dry cleaning firm tell their acquaintances about it and word gets around to the effect that those people at the university can solve almost any problem. This does not hurt the reputation of the university. Actually it helps in getting legislative support and donors to give money to support the good work at the university.

Another type of research is classified research. Usually this type of research is done under government contract and is classified, which means it is to be kept secret from all except those who requested it. The government officials who determined it should be classified did so because they were convinced that the national security justified it.

The federal government supports the largest part of university research. The money comes from the Department of Defense, Health and Welfare, Education, Atomic Energy, the National Science Foundation, and the National Aeronautics and Space Administration.

In 1965 the federal government started a cost-sharing system in its allocation of money to the universities for research. This called for the university to put up approximately five percent of the amount of money that the government made available with each grant. The exception to the five-percent rule or requirement has been the National Science Foundation which expects the university to put up more than five percent. The federal government officials made this ruling in order to get the university officials to pay more attention to the research work being done under government grants with the expectation that such would get better results.

Federal government rules concerning research grants require substantiation by an authorized university official of charges made for time spent on research.

The university usually requires quarterly reports on sponsored research. These usually include the status of and future plans for the technical details of the research and the staffing, as well as updated fiscal information concerning remaining funds.

As a matter of fact, universities require those in the university who are receiving pay to do research to report weekly, bimonthly, or on each payday the amount of time and when he worked on the project.

Some research people at the universities give full time to research and others give part time to research and other time to consulting and/or teaching. Some universities allocate a specified amount of money to new teachers for devoting half time to research. The idea here is to give the teacher an opportunity to do some research, publish an article or so, and thus enhance his reputation in his field of specialization.

Research is big business in universities. It cannot be left to chance. The research work of a university is administered by an office for research administration or a dean of research or a director of research.

Each research office should have a manual of information for principal investigators. It should describe the local ground rules governing the acquisition of research support and the rules governing the operation of the research program, including the procurement of personnel, once support is secured.

The preparation of proposals for research consumes much time. It is an art based on knowledge. Some people are good at it and others need not even try. The latter could be an excellent research person. He should get help from others who are adept at it when he gets ready to prepare a proposal. Knowing the people who have the responsibility of approving or disapproving the proposal has something to do with the outcome. The reputation of the person in research has much to do with the response to the proposal. Sometimes to young people in research it appears that "the rich get richer and the poor get poorer," but the young ones who stick with it usually get better and all of the older ones eventually retire or die.

The attitude of the university toward research has much to do with the quality of research done in any given university. The writer has two degrees from Yale and not any from Harvard. However, he received an appointment to be a Research Associate at Harvard for one summer, and during that summer he discovered one of the reasons why even Yale has difficulty at times in overcoming Harvard. The attitude of all of the people at Harvard with whom the writer came in contact was definitely to enhance research and push back the boundaries of knowledge. There was a clear and concise statement of what was wanted in the research work. Then there was freedom and open doors. The people at the greatest

80

university library in the world went out of their way in clearing the way for the writer's research. The general idea at the library was come and get the knowledge and do not permit any technicalities to stand in your way. If you need help in clearing away any obstructions, let us know and we will get them out of your way. The authorities at the university realized that researchers need some recreation or diversions to keep their brains working at top speed. They provided the writer with free tickets to concerts and free use of tennis courts. There was little time for socializing, but the association with other people doing research work at that time was stimulating. These people were "go-getters" and there was no question about it. It felt almost like a race to see which person would get to the finish line first.

There has been some concern on the part of thoughtful people that so much emphasis on organized research in universities would ruin the universities. This concern takes two forms. The first is that the grants from outside the university for specified research might not be in keeping with the objectives or well-being of the university, and eagerness to get the money might overshadow the potential damage. There is some danger here. Inconsequential research could amount to a waste of time. Research in certain areas could result in answers that are politically unpopular. However, fact is fact and truth is truth wherever it is found, and it should be defended until further research reveals greater truths.

The second concern is that too much emphasis on organized research in a given university might detract from the effectiveness of the teaching. Research is more prestigious than teaching, in the minds of most university faculty members. The reason is that research results in publication and publications are given great weight in determining rank and salary. Often grants pay more than regular salaries and faculty members are not allergic to such. Yes, there is danger in permitting a situation where research dominates and teaching is secondary. However, a university is committed to teaching, research, and service, and a satisfactory balance among the three is one of the duties of the administration and the board of control.

University presses were established beginning in 1869 at Cornell to facilitate the publication of research work.

University presses have been up against the odds in trying to sell scholarly reports of research. In order to make ends meet financially many of them have printed other types of books that gave promise of having a larger sales volume.

The writer initiated the establishment of a university press in one state. It required about six years of consistent and persuasive work. It is difficult to get much support for a university press other than on the campuses. Often board members think of it as an unnecessary extra. Legislators had rather put money somewhere else. One emphasis that helped set the stage for establishing the university press was the emphasis in that state on research and development, which was designated to bring more industry to the state. However, when professors discussed the type of research they expected to have published by the press, it was difficult for nonacademicians to see any relationship between that and the well-being of the state.

Another factor that delayed the establishment of the press was the fact that the writer was the president of one of the state-supported universities under the central board of trustees and some of the people in the other seven universities and some of the trustees thought the writer would control the operation of the press, thus making the other seven universities of secondary importance in the whole thing. However, eventually through the combined efforts of many people, the press was established.

A very competent person was found to head the press and after much struggling the press became fairly well-established, even though it had to and still does publish some nonscholarly books. However, the important point is that the press definitely stimulated more research on all eight of the state-supported campuses and at private colleges and universities in the area.

University presses have been of great value in motivating creativity among university faculty members, and they should continue to do so.

Universities believe in the advancement of knowledge and have pioneered in such. Outstanding work in basic research by university faculty members is essential in bettering our way of life, which is one of the objectives of higher education.

Quality control in research comes from the nature of the proposals when faculty teaching loads are reduced to provide time for research. These proposals are usually checked carefully by a committee of faculty members who are working in the subject matter area in which the proposal is made and by the Director of Research in the university.

Quality control in research also comes from publication and feedback. Usually if the research is published in a journal or book that is a mark of the work being of high quality. Then the comments or reviews by others--especially those who are knowledgeable about the subject--are very important in judging the quality of the research.

Contract research has conditions attached that are thought to be helpful in getting desired results and if the offer of the contract is accepted by the professor and the university this becomes a control and hopefully one of quality.

Public Service

Go to the university for the answer. This is a common answer given by many people when others need more knowledge or know-how. It would surprise the average citizen to know how many calls of this kind are received by colleges and universities. Even the president gets many such calls as well as complaints! The president of one university got so many calls at home that he had it arranged in such a way that when someone called his published home telephone number, the campus police would answer and determine whether they should "disturb" the president with the call. This president said this arrangement proved to be quite a shock to some tipsy alumni who called him at two o'clock in the morning to complain about the football team not winning the game the previous Saturday.

It is worthwhile to have the public feel that just anyone can call on the college or university for knowledge. It is time-consuming, but it is worth the effort.

Higher education has been called upon for leadership since the colleges were founded in this country. Recently the president of one university got a leave of absence to serve as secretary of Health, Education, and Welfare. More recently a professor at another university got a leave of absence to serve as Secretary of State. Some of these people return to their jobs and others do not.

Key personnel from the institutions of higher learning serve the public in many other ways. Some of them obtain leaves of absence to serve in different types of positions in state government. Some agree to part-time consultant work while holding their regular jobs at the institution.

Some universities render a service to many people by having business bureaus and the like. These bureaus do research and put out reports periodically to those who are interested. This is designed to help people advance in the field. In business, for instance, the objective of the people working at the bureau could be to raise the per-capita income of the state or area from which the university gets support allocations.

Some businesses and industries call on the university to do contracted applied research. This is not basic research, but it is a service to the public.

Service also means that the university is extending its

educational services to those who cannot go to the institution for regular residence instruction. This was mentioned earlier as branch campuses. The leading public universities in some states have vied with each other to see which one could establish the greatest number of such centers. As a result students can receive college instruction within just a few miles from home, if not just across the street.

Actually if a high school graduate has a favorite chair or just any chair in which to sit at home, he does not have to leave it in order to receive college credit. He can get it by means of television.

Systematic efforts along this line started in this country in 1885 at Johns Hopkins University. In the beginning this effort was done through extension committees and departments. Tremendous strides were made in this area of university extension work beginning in 1914 when the federal government began partially financing cooperative agricultural and home economics extension work carried on by land-grant colleges and universities.

The term "university extension" is now sometimes called "extension work," "continuing education," "public service," "community service," etc. When such terms are used they refer to credit or noncredit work done by college or university personnel off campus except at off-campus centers. However, some of this work especially in continuing education for adults is done on the campuses.

This extension work consists of: extension classes anywhere, home-study or correspondence courses, short courses, discussion groups, seminars, workshops, courses by radio and television, club work, etc.

All of this might sound inconsequential to some people but it exists in every state in the union and in one state the continuing studies programs reach almost a half million people. In another state where the writer lived and worked at one time it reaches one hundred thousand people. This emphasis has grown out of projected declining enrollments because of the decline in birthrates. Now university planners anticipate their main source of future usefulness is in the area of community service, which really isn't confined to the immediate community. It extends to the state lines, usually with public universities, but it will go anywhere in this country or in the world as long as it can be financed.

The above has caused an editor of a respected periodical to declare that there has been a revolution in higher education in this country and now the American universities have come into their own.

84

Maybe so and maybe not! The continuing increase in the scope and size of extension services certainly will cause fundamental changes in the conception and structure of U.S. universities.

If this "back-to-school" movement results in a wide upgrading in the national culture, it will be worth any change in the concept and structure of American higher education.

There could be some trouble. We claim that we like a competitive society. We claim that we like to cooperate. In reality we like competition and we like to cooperate only when it does not interfere with letting us have what we want. Institutions want more students anywhere so that they can get more money from them and from state appropriations that are based primarily on credit hours earned. Institutions want to give credit for the course or experience, rather than have it listed as a noncredit enterprise, so that it will generate more money. This means that some colleges and universities are giving credit for work that is under a baccalaureate-level caliber. Of course, this is perfectly all right for junior colleges that are offering certificates. However, some of this extension work by four-year colleges and universities is at the level of vocational education at the high school level. This is not a function of higher education and if it continues, it will erode the quality standards and result in the decline or demise of higher education in this country.

Usually in this country we try to carry things too far and in such extensions we defeat our own purposes, and this could be the outcome of extension work in American higher education.

The structure of higher education is not of great importance except to the strict traditionalist. The important thing is to keep the value or quality of what is done in higher education at the point where it produces people who can cope and cope successfully with current and future problems and opportunities of their times.

Professional accrediting agencies run by educators have an awful time safeguarding quality and standards in extension work. Extension work and off-campus centers will be given careful scrutiny in the future. Therefore, some of them will be changed drastically in what they offer and some of them will be discontinued. However, it is essential for higher education to devote some time to public service, but not to the extent of weakening instruction and research.

Quality control in public service comes from checking carefully to see that the people doing the work are competent. Then the quality of the work can be determined by the results. If the work has been effective the people for whom the work was done can say so, and they can make requests for repeat performances if needed.

Chapter 6

SUPPORT SERVICES AND ACTIVITIES

In this chapter there will be a discussion of the library, guidance, extra-curricula activities, intercollegiate athletics, and auxiliary enterprises.

Library

College and university libraries started in this country in 1638 with John Harvard's collection of 260 volumes. Now the Harvard library has a collection of items numbering over seven million, and has more items in it than any college or university in this country.

A college or university library has in it books, periodicals, maps, government documents, microfilms, films, recordings, audio tapes, video tapes, museum objects, and special collections. The special collections could include rare books, books and other materials on local history, braille books, talking books, etc. Some libraries offer instructional television, programmed learning, independent study, etc.

The building in which the library is located should be designed for the purpose for which it was intended and by experts who know library work and construction of libraries. Consultants should be obtained for this purpose because competent ones are well worth the money invested. The reason for getting consultants is because so many people on the campus think they know exactly what is needed, and a consultant can pool the various points of view expressed on the campus and relate them to his knowledge of library work and to the projected needs of the future. The writer had the responsibility and privilege of constructing a new library at a university where he was president, and the first thing that he did even before he got the money to finance it was to have his associates make an international survey of library consultants. The head librarian of Harvard University was chosen for the job, and it was a joy to work with such a competent person. The library was constructed under his supervision, and it has served well.

It is very important to have an extremely competent person as head or chief librarian. There has been considerable debate in academic circles in regard to whether the library staff professionals should be members of the faculty. They should be if they have the qualifications to meet the standards in effect in the local institution for the various ranks. The head librarian should have the qualification for the rank of full professor and should have that rank. There are not many people with Ph.D.

degrees in library science. Only a handful of universities offer such degrees and they have very few students pursuing such degrees. Ideally a head librarian should have a doctor of philosophy degree in library science, but there are not enough to go around. Some institutions settle for a person who has a doctorate in some subject-matter field and a master's degree in library science. Many libraries have head librarians with lesser qualifications, and of course they should have lower faculty ranks. In these cases sometimes it is better not to give the head librarian faculty rank, because he will be working with full professors and he can be more effective when he is of equal rank. One of the most important jobs in higher education is that of the head librarian, and every possible effort should be made to get the very best that is in existence. It is better to have an acting head for a short while than to settle for someone who does not have the experience and qualifications desired.

The library staff is usually organized into specialized departments. The large departments are cataloging, circulation, and reference. Some of the other classifications are reader's services, acquisitions, reserve books, rare books, etc.

Every institution has a library committee. The membership of the committee rotates yearly or more often so that all of the departments in the institution can have representation on the committee. Some departments in some institutions battle continuously for the purchase of additional books and periodicals in their fields of expertise. Therefore, the library committees act only in an advisory capacity. Usually, the book selections are made jointly with representatives from the faculty and from the professional library staff, but the final decisions are left to the head librarian, and that is one of the reasons why the head librarian should be so very competent.

A collection of books becomes a library when it is organized. The card catalogs record everything in the library according to authors and subjects. Some items in the library are for reference and may not be checked out of the library. They are to help people find what they want. Some books are on the reserve shelves. These may be checked out for a restricted period of time so that all of the members of the class may use them before the time period as assigned by the teacher expires. Other books may be checked out of the library by those who are authorized to do so which usually are students, faculty members, administrators, and staff members. However, college and university libraries should be available to noncollege-connected people so long as such does not interfere with its use by the campus community.

Some of the libraries have closed stacks and others have open stacks. Most of them have open stacks. The writer visited and used an open-stack library at a university in the city where this paragraph is being written--the University of Miami. He had access to the reference books, the card catalog, and the books and periodicals throughout the library. He went up in the stacks and got the books that he wanted and sat in a cubicle and read the books until he obtained the information that he wanted, and then he left the library. He had every privilege as a visitor that any member of the student body or faculty had except to check out books. This is an extremely valuable service to people who are in the community. This did not cost the writer anything even though this experience took place at a private rather than a public-supported university.

At one time the writer lived in a city where there were eight colleges and universities. In this city there was a joint university library system. All of those connected with any one of the colleges and universities in the city had full access to any one of the libraries in the city. This cuts the cost of collections and makes the range of information or knowledge available in the city much greater. The system there is Nashville, Tennessee, has been a model for other joint adventures in cities throughout the nation.

College and university libraries make interlibrary loans. A student at one university can call for and get a book from another university if the library in the university where he is enrolled does not have it. Loans from these libraries are also made to public libraries.

A few institutions have added as many as one hundred thousand volumes to their libraries in a given year. This is unusual and the money has to come from some special source. For instance, a legislature could appropriate special catch-up funds to an institution in order to meet accrediting association requirements. Or a donor could make the money available to a private university to strengthen its holdings in a certain field of study.

College and university library financing is on a much smaller scale than mentioned in the preceding paragraph. The library budget is usually about five percent of the educational and general budget of the institution, and only approximately forty percent of this amount is spent on books, periodicals, binding, supplies, equipment, and travel. The other sixty percent goes for salaries and wages. This is an incredibly small amount going for books and periodicals to update the library. That is the reason why librarians and college and university administrators try to get money for their libraries from other sources.

Some federal funds are available to higher education libraries. Some money is available to purchase books and periodicals under Title II of the Higher Education Act of 1965, Public Law 89-329. Also under Title IV money is available for audiovisual materials and equipment in college and university libraries. Medical school libraries can obtain federal funds under the Medical Library Assistance Act, Public Law 89-291.

Still there is not enough money available for the libraries. Some of the institutions have formed "Friends of the Library" organizations. The purpose of these organizations is to get individuals, businesses and industry to make special grants to the library.

An institution of higher learning cannot have a high rating if it does not have a good library. The reason for this is that the library is the place where the teacher keeps up-to-date and where the students go to learn more about what the teacher told them in class. Adequate learning cannot take place without an adequate library. An illustration of this is off-campus instruction. It cannot be as effective when students do not have access to a good library. But most often the same credit is given for off-campus instruction as is given for on-campus instruction, and that is one reason why the trend to the back-to-school-at-home movement is headed for trouble and probably will cause a crisis in higher education.

A library is a good one when it has all of the books, periodicals, films, slides, phonograph records, and tapes, etc., that the students need to explore the subjects taught to the extent as required by the teachers. To have the books and materials to go beyond the teachers' requirements would be excellent. To have all that the teachers want for their own professional reading would make the library super.

The increase in knowledge is developing so rapidly that many new volumes must be acquired for the library every year, and access to volumes in other libraries by electronic methods must be expanded.

Hijacking books is common at college and university libraries, as well as at all other types of libraries. A recent cartoon showed the librarian at a public library holding a little boy while she talked by phone to his mother. The librarian told the mother, "I have your son here as hostage and I am going to hold him until you return the library's book." Some libraries have gates through which a person has to go in order to check out books or even to get out of the library. They are similar to the gates through which people must go to board a commercial plane. Fines are assessed for the loss of books. Fines are assessed for the late return of books. Almost every conceivable thing has been tried to cut down on or eliminate the loss and late return of books and no one seems to know an adequate answer.

The ideal is to have as free access to the contents of the

library as possible in such a way as not to have an excessive loss and to have check-outs returned on time. There are many reasons why the ideal is not achieved. People who are in colleges and universities are of a higher stripe intellectually speaking, but they are not necessarily of a higher stripe from an ethical point of view. Even though colleges and universities have some of all types, the problem of losses and late returns at libraries is not necessarily because students and teachers want to steal or to be late in returning something. The problem seems to be centered in procrastination. They simply put off doing what they know they should do until it is too late to do it on time. The cure, as stated above, is not known, but the solution must be based on a campus-wide understanding that the losses will cause tuition to be increased.

Very expensive automation is making libraries centers of massive information. The problem for the student will be how to sift out the information that he wants. Undoubtedly guidelines on this will be issued periodically.

The quality controls of the libraries come from three major sources. The American Library Association has standards that must be met if the library is approved by that association. The Regional Accrediting Agency has standards for the library that must be met if the institution is to be accredited by the agency. The institution library committee makes recommendations for the improvement of the quality of the library.

Guidance

Guidance—next to teaching and research—could be the most important part of higher education. Guidance can provide direction and motivation. Most students need one or both at some time during their college careers. When students are making good progress, they are satisfied enough to stay in college. When they want to stay in college, they work better for their teachers. More money comes in for the college or university when they remain enrolled. Thus, the institution is in position to meet expenses and make progress—assuming, of course, that the other sources of income are producing adequate funds.

One of the most haphazard things in existence is the choice of majors by college students. Some college students made up their minds early concerning what they want to get out of college, but most of them do not and have not at the time of entrance. They say they want a college education because their peers are getting one. Or they want a college education to get a good job. Or they want a college education to be better fitted for life.

To make matters even worse, often they choose the wrong college. Some secondary-school guidance officers help some

91

students choose the right college for them and sometimes help them choose a major that is in keeping with their aptitudes and interests.

Let us assume that the college-bound student has chosen the college that he wants to attend and has met the entrance requirements for it, but does not know what he wants as his major. This condition could be considered typical. He could make arrangements to go to that college's guidance department for help prior to the opening date of college. There he could be given aptitude and interest tests and information about careers. If from that it appears that he has chosen the wrong college, it is unlikely that he will be told so. However, this is not too bad because most colleges and universities today are multipurpose institutions and could at least get the student started on the best track for him. Then later he could transfer to a college or university that offers a better program in the field in which he wants to major. Also, many institutions of higher learning offer general education during the first two years of college, but a person who wants to major in music, engineering, home economics, etc., finds that the specialization that such curricula often require during the first two years has to be made up and often requires an extra year of college.

Once a student has chosen a course of study he has some direction, but he needs more. Every guidance center in every college and university should see that every undergraduate student has a counselor for his entire four years. It does not have to be the same person. This person's main job is to help the student to meet scholastic standards.

The student is a whole person, and sometimes he cannot meet scholastic requirements and standards because he has personal problems.

The academic counselor is not supposed to deal with personal problems, but the student cannot be cut up into segments. He will discuss some of these with his academic counselor, and this counselor can give advice on them, but it is better for him to ask the student to go to the guidance center and ask for help on such there.

The trouble with academic counselors and other counselors outside of the guidance office is that practically all of them have not had any courses in counseling. However, the guidance office does not have enough personnel to do all of the counseling and, if it did, the academic department heads would not want them to do academic counseling anyway. This means that all department heads should give specific instruction to each member of the department who is assigned students for academic counseling.

92

Academic department heads or academic deans or both should check each student's program of study each term to determine whether the academic counseling or the student's follow-through was in error in any way. Most institutions do not do this each term or even the term just prior to scheduled graduation time. However, it is good business to do it because it pays off in better-satisfied customers. It avoids many of the confrontations at scheduled graduation times.

Nonacademic counseling is endless. It covers every possible thing that can happen to young people who are between eighteen and twenty-two years of age. This includes all things that the counselor has studied about or heard about plus some new ones.

Usually guidance centers do not include medical doctors and psychiatrists. Counselors should make referrals to such doctors when students need them. Colleges and universities have arrangements with such doctors to take care of such needs. Some counselors have difficulty making such referrals. In other words, they think they know it all. Such can get the student into even deeper trouble.

The professionally trained guidance counselors should be able to help students solve all of their problems except those that are medical, and very complicated mental problems.

Many of the student problems never get to the guidance officer. One of the writer's first jobs was director of Varsity Hall at Pennsylvania State University. Here all the male athletes of the university were in residence. They kept coming to me with all kinds of personal problems and I referred some, but tried to take care of the others. My background included a great many courses in student personnel work. One problem, for instance, that came to me had to do with a fellow who some of the football players told me would not leave his room. I told them I would see about it. Before I could get to see the fellow, the football players had picked him up and taken him out on the lawn. I heard a commotion outside and when I looked out of the window, I saw about six huge men pulling on a tall, skinny guy who had his arms locked around a small tree. I upped the window and told them to leave him alone because I was coming down to see him immediately. I went down and got the men to stand back while I talked to the fellow. He wouldn't talk at first and I could tell he was in a deep, depressed state. With his arms still locked around the tree, I finally got him to tell me what was wrong. His father had sold his favorite heifer--one that he had raised from birth. The fellow was from a very fine and deeply religious farm family there in Pennsylvania. I asked him if his father knew that the heifer meant so much to him. He said he didn't know. Then I said, "If I get your father to get that heifer back, will it solve your problem?" He said it would. And I promised him I would try by telephoning his father immediately. This caused him to unlock his arms from around the tree. He went with me to the telephone. I got his father and explained the situation. He said he had no idea that the heifer meant so much to his son and he was sure he could get it back, and he would see about it just as soon as he hung up. He thanked me and told me to assure his son that the heifer would be back in the barn by dark that day. I thanked him and then gave the message to his son. I heard nothing more from the son or the father, but the football players who reported the fellow told me that I must have some sort of magic about me. I did not tell them differently!

Sometimes in counseling, as in all of life, a counselor has to work against time. In the above instance it was a matter of getting a fellow back in class and in mental condition to win the next football game. Getting the heifer back was the shortcut. I could have told him that he was growing up and he should be able to take such disappointments in stride, and he should unlock his arms from around that tree and get up like a man and go ahead about his business as a student and an athlete. This approach would have taken longer and in all probability it would have been successful. On the other hand, that approach could have resulted in the student's dropping out of college and worse yet (for the alumni/ae!) Penn State could have had a losing football season.

So often residence directors at colleges and universities are selected on the basis of the person who will cost the least amount of money, one who can keep down the noise, and one who can keep students from tearing or breaking up the place. Actually, the job of being a residence director is a very important job in that usually this person is the first official in the institution to hear about or be given the opportunity to work with the student about his problem. They should be trained counselors either through having completed courses in guidance or through guidance training given by guidance officers at the institution. The office of dean of students should do this or see that is done by very competent people.

I served as faculty advisor of one of the fraternities at Penn State. I enjoyed it very much, and there I learned at least two things in my counseling of students.

One might think members of a fraternity would be very much alike. Undoubtedly they are more alike than students chosen at random. However, even among fraternity brothers I learned that each student is somewhat different from all other students. This I tried to remember throughout my professional career working with students.

The second thing that I learned was that students can be motivated. I guess I should have know this, but it was my first

94

job and I wanted all those things I had learned in books to be demonstrated. I found that more learning takes place in an atmosphere of security and belonging. Also, I found out that more learning takes place when a student feels a need for it. Our fraternity won the top academic trophy and many other types of trophies. I was very proud of those men.

Guidance can get better results than is suspected by many people. It is absolutely essential in higher education in order to more nearly approximate human potential.

The quality control in guidance or counseling is that at least one person in the guidance center must be licenses by the State License Board. All reports that are issued from the guidance office must be signed by a licensed member of the guidance center staff. Counselors who meet the standards of a national certification association may receive such a certificate, but employment in a college or university guidance center usually does not require the certificate.

Extracurricular Activities

Extracurricular activities are designed to train students for responsible citizenship and leadership.

All students should be encouraged to participate in one or more extracurricular activities. Of course, no student can be compelled to participate in extracurricular activities. But to participate helps in developing a well-rounded adjustment to life. A campus is a community and functions very much like a township or small city. Most graduates will live in similar places and can learn through participation in extracurricular activities much of what to do and how to go about getting things done as citizens after college.

Taking part in extracurricular activities is participatory democracy. Students learn when they participate. They learn under expert guidance from staff members and faculty advisers. A college campus is not quite an adult community, and mistakes made on campuses do not carry the kind of penalty that are metered out in a township or city. Some people learn from mistakes they make and they are not likely to make the same mistake after graduation that they made in college. Someone has said that if a person makes the same mistake more than once, he is dumb, and college graduates are not supposed to be dumb.

No student should be permitted to participate in extracurricular activities to the extent that such participation interferes with his studies or his health. A few students enjoy participating in extracurricular activities so much that it appears that they are majoring in extracurricular activities.

Some of these people actually flunk out of college. Others level off to the extent that they meet graduation requirements, and many of them get jobs that require the same abilities as those used in being successful in extracurricular activities.

The trick to it is for the student to select a few extracurricular activities in which to participate and do them well rather than trying to get into just as many as he can.

Those students who are trying to make athletic teams often find that they cannot participate in any of the extracurricular activities and still pass their work. Some of them, however, have the ability and find the time to pass their courses, be on an athletic team or teams, and take part in extracurricular activities.

Students should be expected to accept responsibility for as much of the extracurricular leadership as they can carry under trained adult supervision. Participate and then lead--that is the story of our democracy and there is no better place to learn how to do it than on a college campus. Leadership in college usually leads to leadership after graduation. There are some late bloomers who show such metal later on. There are some who are not interested in leading in college and become leaders later on. And, of course, some of the college leaders do not turn out very well.

Participation in student government is a responsibility but it is great training in leadership. Student government functions with adult supervision or guidance, but all positions are held by elected students. Some committee memberships are appointive. Student government should see that student conduct should not interfere with the rights and development of other students and not reflect unfavorably upon the college. Further, it should assure fair treatment and justice to each student. Student governments sponsor all kinds of projects, and assist the college in many ways as it strives to achieve its goals. For instance, student government teams have successfully lobbied for college funds with legislators in the capitol.

Many of the extracurricular activities are designed to develop the student socially, physically, and religiously.

Social life centers around whatever is the "in" thing to do. Gatherings of all kinds are promoted. Some emphasize dancing, some listening to music, some singing, etc. Students learn how to put on receptions, plan pep rallies, and the like.

Religious development is usually headed up by the Student Religious Association. Most campuses have a chapel and services are held here periodically. Usually there is no proselyting.

Each student is encouraged to grow in his or her own religious affiliation or faith. Many colleges and universities employ a chaplain and he is there not only to participate in services but also to have private conferences with students who desire help in their religious development. Some religious organizations have centers on the campuses or nearby and they have programs and help the students in their religious development. Student Christian Associations are on many campus and they have rendered significant service in helping students in their religious development.

The physical activities are usually headed up by the Student Athletic Association. In conjunction with the Athletic Department every form of athletic recreation is promoted. Intramural athletics has become very popular. This is important in an institution of higher learning because everyone knows that a bright mind cannot function well in a "sick" body.

Usually institutions have a publications board made up of students, faculty, and administrators. Policies for the student publications are determined by these boards. Complaints about the operation of the newspaper, yearbook, and other student publications are heard and usually solved by such boards. Much concern has centered around student newspapers and yearbooks. Some alumni/ae have complained that some yearbooks have included too much sex. Some administrators have claimed that some of the newspapers have listed so many exaggerated complaints about the institution that they have hurt the reputation or image of the institution. These are just some of the examples of the types of complaints leveled against student publications. It should be remembered that student publications are just that--student publications. These people are in the process of growing up. They are not perfect and neither are their supervisors. Also, it must be remembered that often people shortly forget what was put in print yesterday or even today. Nevertheless, all publications should be kept in line by the publications board in regard to facts, truth, and sincere beliefs that are typical of the members of the student body.

Student desires are given careful consideration in the cultural program that takes place on the college campus. Lectures, exhibits, and concerts take place on every college campus. The artist course series is an important extracurricular activity because it contributes in a significant way to the development of the well-rounded student.

Departmental clubs are active in promoting interest in and the participation of departmental work. Art departments sponsor exhibits of student and nonstudent work. Drama departments produce plays. Business departments have conferences on work with computers. And so it goes with much credit because here the students can participate in and see the practical application of

97

what they learn in the classroom.

Honor societies are found on every campus. Students who do well in their academic studies are tapped by these societies. Examples are Phi Beta Kappa, Tau Beta Pi, Phi Kappa Phi, American Society of Civil Engineers, and the like. Membership in such is a great honor. These groups meet periodically and have programs to advance interest in their respective specializations.

One of the joys of administration is to see how really responsible student leaders can be. Of course, at any time any institution can have a crop of student leaders who leave much to be desired. However, student leaders are elected by their peers and most of them are responsible and effective, and this reflects favorably on those who elected them.

Earlier this week the writer visited the president of the University of Miami and learned about two incidents that involved out-of-classroom student activities.

The president was interested in raising faculty salaries to help offset inflation. He decided that the only way in which this could be done was to raise tuition. He made his proposal to his board of trustees and when it became known on the campus, the students or at least some of the student leaders vigorously disagreed. A large peaceful demonstration followed. A compromise was being considered. Then during the controversy one of the student leaders made a constructive proposal. He proposed that the students receive only one-half of the tuition rebate for the second semester if the tuition income exceeded the budgetary estimates and if this amount of money would be spent on campus improvements. This proposal was approved by the student senate, the president, and the board of trustees. The result was the expenditure of $450,000 on campus improvements.

The president of this university is retiring after serving twenty years as president of this institution. He has already been given an appreciation dinner and along with other gifts he received two plaques of appreciation from two past student leaders whom the president actually had had removed by the police from the Administration Building on separate occasions.

Collective student leadership is powerful. The writer, as president of a university, met once a month with the president's council. This council consisted of the twelve elected student presidents of the twelve largest student organizations on the campus. Anything could get on the agenda of these meetings from any member of the council or from the president of the university. The meetings were very informal. The students liked this arrangement because they had input at the very top of the university. The president of the university liked the arrangement because through this group he could keep in close touch with the wishes and needs of the students. The president of the university found that the members of this council could get almost anything done among the students on the campus. The president of the university in many instances did not even have to make requests. All he had to do was to express his wishes or desires and the members of the council would get busy and see that they were realized. This resulted from the mutual feeling that everyone really cared and wanted to do everything they could to help the students get a good education, develop into responsible citizens and leaders, and enjoy the process.

Students must have some release from their studying. If institutions of higher education did not have extracurricular programs, students would find some other form of diversion, which could be destructive. Therefore, some form of an extracurricular activities program is essential, and such is not very expensive.

The Student Government Association has standards by which extracurricular activities must be conducted. The administrative officials of the institution have sponsors, advisers etc. to help guide the form that the activities take.

Intercollegiate Athletics

Our University Planning Council at Florida State University started intercollegiate football at that university. The football team of that university accepted a bid to play in the Orange Bowl on New Years Day, 1981. Was starting it an achievement or a mistake?

It is claimed that skills are developed in intercollegiate athletics, and that is no doubt true. It is claimed that character is developed in intercollegiate football, but when the public saw on national television the head coach of one of the bowl teams use his fists on the player of the opposing team because he made the play that defeated the head coach's team, I am not sure about how much character is developed in intercollegiate athletics. That head coach got away with it. This is the opposite of developing good character.

The desire to win is with most of us, but in intercollegiate athletics it becomes so intense that some people in it or associated with the institution or graduates or dropouts of the institution will be anything to win.

There is one good aspect of the intense desire to win, and it is that one institution will observe a rival intensely to find a violation that he can report. Here the regional conferences and the National Collegiate Athletic Association (NCAA) are of great assistance. They investigate the reports and if found to be accurate they impose penalties on the offending teams and institutions.

These associations serve other useful purposes. They set the limits for the number and amount of remuneration that can be offered in any given institution for each sport. They set eligibility standards for participation in each sport. This supervision started in 1905 when President Theodore Roosevelt urged the formation of such when there was a move to abolish football because players were being injured and killed.

Everyone knows that there are injuries and a few deaths in intercollegiate athletics. An injury the family can live with because the offspring took the chance. A death cannot be lived with if the dead one is your son or daughter. Of course, he or she too took the chance, but still someone other than the offspring is never forgiven. There are few deaths and injuries in intercollegiate athletics compared with those among students in automobile accidents.

Another problem with intercollegiate athletics is that it is difficult for some of the athletes to meet entrance standards and retain a scholastic average high enough to remain enrolled in college. Some get in on the basis of fraudulent papers. Some get others to take tests for them. Most of them actually meet the entrance standards, but it is another thing for them to make good grades. These athletes are given more guidance and counseling than any other students in the university. They are guided into courses that are more in keeping with their interests. Some say they take only "crip" courses. This is not true, but many of them take courses that are easier to pass than most courses in college. The difficulty with the situation is the athlete has to give so very much of his time to training and traveling to meet the schedule of games off campus that he is not in class enough to profit from what the teacher has to offer. Some of the athletes graduate, but many of them do not. Some of those who hope to make professional teams and do not state that they have been cheated in that even though they have the degree, they do not have an education. This could be sour grapes or based on fact. Administrators give endless time to this problem and they do their very best to create a situation where the athlete can get an education and the teams can win.

Another problem connected with intercollegiate athletics is that it is so very expensive. The general public usually has attention focused on the top collegiate teams and does not see the small college or university which has practically no receipts from admission to contests and no income from local games. From tuition the salaries of physical education teachers are paid and from there on the money should come from some other place, but usually more comes from the general budget of the institution.

Alumni of these institutions usually give very little to the athletic association because the institution has so few winning teams. Even if these institutions have intercollegiate athletic teams that win in their classification, it is not quite the same to the alumni/ae and general public as winning in the top bracket of the NCAA.

Some smaller institutions try to solve the problem by concentrating on one sport or just a few sports where they think they have a good chance of excelling. Here they recruit as fiercely as the big ones, and often they come up with the prizes.

Athletic recruiting is a science and an art. The amount of information accumulated about athletes of exceptional ability is astounding. The institution's recruiters leave nothing to guesswork. They really know the prospective athletic enrollee inside and out. Persuasion is a factor, and a major one, in successful recruiting. Of course the track record of the institution in athletics has more weight but people including athletes like attention and they really get it if they have made a good athletic record in secondary school.

Intercollegiate athletics is a contradiction. If there is not a winning record, the coaches are fired. Without a continuity of coaching--a sort of dynasty--winning teams are not produced. Of course, there are exceptions to this, but it is the general rule. The firings generally are instigated by the alumni/ae. Some alumni/ae are fanatics when it comes to intercollegiate athletics, especially football. They want a winning team all of the time and so does everyone else, but somebody on the schedule has to lose unless all games result in ties. When an institution has a losing season or two or three in a given sport, what recourse is there other than to fire the coach? The athletic director could be fired. The president of the institution could be fired. But usually the easiest of these to fire is the coach.

Women in sports has been an issue of late. One institution not far from where this paragraph is being written stands to lose forty million dollars per year in federal grants for allegedly not putting an equal amount of money into athletics for women as it has in athletics for men. This complaint was filed by only one student, but that is all it takes to instigate an investigation. Of course, the institution will have a chance to defend its action at the hearing.

Women are now fully equal in the NCAA. They are in intercollegiate athletics to stay, and all of it comes down to the bottom line in intercollegiate athletics as it does in everything else in higher education, and that is: all are to be treated alike and given the same opportunities.

The band is usually associated with intercollegiate athletics especially football. Of course, the band is more than football. It is more than intercollegiate athletics. It is more than intramural athletics. It is a skill. It is an art. It is music. Practically every secondary school has a band and many college students are ready for this training and activity.

Some institutions put so much emphasis on the band that they call it "The Million Dollar Band." Either it brings to the events enough extra people to increase the institution's income by a million dollars or it could cost someone a million dollars. The athletic association pays the cost of sending the band and cheerleaders to out-of-town games. Most people think the spirit that a band adds to a football game helps the team to win; and, even if not, to see the pretty girls who parade in front of the band at half time is worth the price!

A winning intercollegiate athletic team can galvanize everyone together more than anything else connected with higher education. This is no mean accomplishment. That sort of thing is needed, but it is so very transitory. It is so sweet one year and so sad the next, except in rare cases. The deadening effect of having teams that lose is frustrating for those who are connected with the institution. Of course, some students pay no attention to the intercollegiate athletic program and care less.

Is intercollegiate athletics higher education? I was president of a university when one of our athletic teams won the national basketball championship. Such exhilaration was never before seen or experienced on that campus. A few were injured, no one was killed, and we won. In my contacts with the public, practically nothing other than the national championship was discussed for years. Yes, it was a handle--an opener--but for awhile rarely could I get the conversation with most of the people beyond that point and ont higher education.

At one time intercollegiate athletics was a sideline of higher education. Now it is a major crop. Some people can remember the time when cotton was the major crop for farmers in certain sections of our country. Then came the boll weevil. The boll weevil meant devastation to the cotton crop before chemicals were found to control and destroy them. The boll weevil caused the farmer to diversify. Now many of them have soybeans as a major crop. And so it is with intercollegiate athletics and higher education. The soybeans have not replaced the cotton yet. Intercollegiate athletics has not replaced higher education yet. But some people in Alabama were so pleased with the diversification of crops that they built and dedicated a statue of a boll weevil in commemoration of his contribution to the financial well-being of farmers and this statue still stands today.

Intercollegiate athletics is a business. It is a major crop. Possibly higher education can discover other major crops and develop all of them to the point where they can contribute to the cost of financing higher education. If so, then we should erect a statue to someone, just as the lowly boll weevil has been so honored.

The way that the boll weevil did it was to be so very devastating. Maybe higher education can do it in the same way. Higher education has a good start in that it has enormously costly medical schools and hospitals, enormously expensive intercollegiate athletic programs, etc.

Several years ago, with tongue in cheek, a person published an article in a leading magazine entitled "The Demise of Football." It referred to intercollegiate football in American colleges and universities. Interest in this became so intense that alumni and others demanded that institutions schedule two games rather than one each Saturday. For example, the University of Michigan had to schedule a game with Purdue and Nebraska to go on at the same time in stadia that were side by side with tunnels leading from one to the other. All went well until one Saturday afternoon, signals were crossed and teams took to the wrong tunnels, resulting in one University of Michigan team playing other University of Michigan team, and the fans in the capacity-filled stands did not know the difference until the next morning when they read about it in the newspapers. This caused humiliation and disgust, resulting in "For Sale" signs being placed on all football stadia throughout the country.

This could be the end of intercollegiate athletics. However, such does not seem to be on the horizon. On the contrary, the "hold outs" have this year "given in." Emory University, John Hopkins University, and the University of Chicago, which have not had intercollegiate athletics, has now with five other institutions formed an athletic conference to enter the intercollegiate race even though the distance between some of these institutions is much greater than the distance between members of other conferences.

Many people are interested in lessening the emphasis that is placed on intercollegiate athletics. Some of the presidents of colleges and universities are making a move to have more to say about the controls on intercollegiate athletics, but so far the trend toward professionalism has not been checked.

One difficulty in enforcing the rules or regulations or controls seems to be with the Boards of Control of the colleges and universities. Boards, as a rule, want winning teams. NCAA and conferences cannot be everywhere all of the time. Enforcement of rules for athletic programs should ultimately be in the hands of the president of the institution. However, some presidents are reluctant to "take a stand" and enforce the regulations because the average length of tenure of a president is only seven years and they have seen Boards of Control side with the athletic department rather than with the president. In some instances this has resulted in the firing of the president even though the firing is usually enclothed with some of the shortcomings of the president.

Academics must supersede athletics in all colleges and universities otherwise the reason for existence of higher education will be lost, and the quest for quality will be lost.

Boards of control must let it be clearly known that coaches are responsible to the Director of Athletics and the Director of Athletics is responsible not to the board but to the president of the institution even if in some instances it is through one of the president's vice-presidents.

Auxiliary Enterprises

Auxiliary enterprises operated by colleges and universities include residence halls, apartment houses, dining halls and other food services, student stores, laundries, barber and beauty shops, college unions, parking garages and other parking facilities, recreational centers, camps, printing shops, dairy farms, and other similar services. Only three of these will be discussed.

Food Service

Whether the food service is handled by the institution's staff or turned over to outside food agencies, it should be done well. Charges for food should be sufficient to supply an adequate amount of good food, well-prepared, and served in an attractive manner, and within the ability of the students and their parents to pay.

The food serving areas and activities include dining halls, lunch rooms, cafeterias, tea rooms, soda and snack bars, and catering services for conferences, meetings, student activities, public functions, and other events.

National campus dining services are prevalent. If this type of contract service is engaged, the contracts should be written with the institution's interest paramount and with institutional authorities in full control over all policies related to the program.

Food service is difficult to handle. Students often blame the food when they are upset by other matters.

At any rate, frequent reports should be received by the institution's administrators on the number of students served, the number of meals served, the cost per meal served, and the distribution of expenditures.

Controls for health are furnished periodically by inspections made by the State Health Department.

Student Housing

Some colleges and universities do not provide any housing for students. Most of the institutions provide housing of one or more of three types. Large dormitories or dormitory complexes are provided on most campuses and they are designed to house from one hundred to one thousand students. Some of these buildings include their own dining halls and common areas for recreation and study. Some of them are receiving telecommunication equipment.

The second type consists of small-group houses. Most fraternity and sorority houses are in this category. These units usually house from twenty-five to fifty students. These usually have a high degree of student self-management of all aspects of the house. The small-group houses usually have a high degree of community spirit among the residents.

The third type of housing includes apartments or self-contained units. They are common on many campuses, and virtually all married student and family housing is of the apartment variety. Usually there is not any residential educational and counseling in these units.

The Director of a Residence Hall has a responsible job. His or her responsibilities include: selection, training and supervision of student staff, advising resident hall government, coordinating building maintenance and custodial concerns, identifying safety and security problems, interpreting and enforcing university rules and regulations, and performing developmental work as assigned.

The Residence Hall Director strives to foster an environment that promotes academic achievement, personal development, and the physical comfort of the students.

Quality controls for student housing rest with the administrators of the institutions.

Campus Security

Organized campus security began in the United States in 1894 when Yale University organized a campus police department. Now most campuses in this country have highly professional security operations. The reason for this is that educational institutions can experience the same crime and security problems as the outside community. Campuses can have acts of terrorism, extortion, kidnapping for ransom or political motives, the taking of hostages and other criminal acts threatening personal safety. Of particular concern is the safety of students, faculty, administrators and staff even though the safety of buildings and grounds are given careful attention.

The administration and enforcement of parking and traffic regulations are responsibilities of the campus police. All vehicles parking on the campus should be registered with the campus police, and parking and traffic rules should be enforced uniformly for students, faculty, administrators, staff and visitors. Control of access and parking fines are ways of enforcing the regulations.

Some security departments have attempted to protect buildings and critical university areas through automatic intrusion detection and alarm systems. Closed-circuit television, remote locking devices and other electronic intrusion devices are used.

A number of security departments have launched crime prevention programs involving posters, colorful pamphlets, discussions with students, releases to campus newspapers, and talks on campus radio stations. These try to educate the campus community about their security responsibilities.

An excellent campus security department should be a part of every institution of higher learning. The need for this can be seen from the two true stories that follow.

Bomb threats are so very easy to make and are absolutely terrifying. They can be caused by trivial things and of course they can be made by mentally warped individuals. One college president claims that he was certain but could not prove why one bomb threat took place on his campus. He said that one of his security men noticed an off-campus student literally up a tree in front of a classroom building on the campus courting one of the coeds. The security officer was of the opinion that courting should not take place in a tree and ordered them down. The young man, it was reported, was infuriated at the cop's interfering in his private life and threatened to get revenge. The next day the dean's office received an anonymous call saying a bomb had been planted in such and such classroom building (the one that happened to be back of the tree in which the courting took place) and it would go off at three o'clock that afternoon. The president of the college immediately ordered the campus security to call the city experts, and together they searched the building for the bomb. This dismissed classes in that building for the remainder of the day, and word spread through the campus like wildfire. No learning, to speak of, took place on the campus for the remainder of the day. The search for the bomb was completed and no bomb was found. This was announced to the students and classes were resumed the following day. It was assumed that the man in the tree was not a student at the university and the campus security officer did not see the need to get his name or the name of the coed up the tree, so everyone was off scot-free but out of the tree. The losers were the students who did not learn much, if anything, during that time and the administrators who, contrary to the thinking of some people, really care about students and feel they just must take every bomb threat seriously and take action accordingly because the next one just might kill one or more students who would be absolutely innocent victims.

Bomb threats can involve many determined and fanatical people. The president of a university received a telephone call from one of his friends with whom he had often been on hunting trips, and this friend told him that a radical organization in the community did not want the attorney general of the neighboring state to speak on the campus. The president wanted to know why the group wanted the speech cancelled, and his friend told him that the attorney general was the only person who had prosecuted the head of their group and got a conviction and a jail sentence for him. Thus the attorney general was an enemy of the group. The president explained to his friend that freedom of speech was involved and he would like for him to take word to the group to please not interfere with the scheduled speech. The friend said he would take the work to the group and would be back in touch as soon as he could. The next day the president received a telephone call from the same friend who said he took the word to the group but it did not do any good. They wanted the scheduled speech cancelled and if it weren't a bomb would be planted in the auditorium where the speech was to take place, and it would be timed to go off during the speech to kill the attorney general and maybe others who would be nearby. The president asked his friend if he thought the group really would follow through with the threat. He said he was certain those guys would do so with pleasure. The president asked his friend to ask the group to hold everything until he could think it over a little more, and he would be back in touch with him the next day. He agreed to do so. In the meantime the president talked the situation over with campus security and with the members of his board of trustees and also the governor of the state who was called into it by the board for the purpose of determining whether state troops would be available to protect the attorney general and the people who would attend the lecture. The president called his friend the next day and told him to tell the group that to insure freedom of speech on the campus, he would have to permit the scheduled speech to take place and for them please not to do anything that would impair the lives of innocent students. The friend said he would deliver the message, but his friend the president should realize that his life

107

could be in danger.

With the consent of the board of trustees, the governor sent state troops to meet the attorney general at the state line and escort him to the university campus. Also the governor sent enough state troops in plain clothes to go to the lecture and disperse themselves in such a way as to smother anyone who might have brought any concealed explosives or weapons into the lecture auditorium. Of course, the explosive experts of the city and state along with campus security had searched the auditorium for any bombs prior to the lecture. The attorney general made his speech. No bomb went off. No other weapon was in evidence. No one was hurt. The state troops escorted the attorney general back to the state line and he is still in good health, and so is the president of the university.

Quality control should be rigidly applied to the selection of campus security officers and their work should meet the standards of performance at all times. This would be an improvement at most colleges and universities.

Chapter 7

OTHER ESSENTIALS

This chapter will include a discussion of buildings and grounds, alumni/ae, public relations, standards and worth.

Buildings and Grounds

More often than not the head of a college or university is confronted by these three questions: How's your football team doing? How many students do you have enrolled? Have you built any new buildings lately?

It is rather difficult for the general public to see how much learning is taking place at an institution of higher learning, but a quick ride through the campus--even the largest ones--can determine the physical growth of an institution. "Ah! That president is a builder. He can get the money. He has a touch of magic about him." Yes, that is a compliment that not all, but some, presidents receive. However, it is still a means toward the end. But often the end of maximum learning could not have been achieved without it. Maximum learning is possible when the institution is competitive. It must have dormitories, student centers, classrooms, libraries, etc., in good condition to attract capable students and the enrollment that is needed to get enough money to attract a competent faculty, and without a competent faculty maximum learning cannot be achieved.

One of the most important aspects of grounds and buildings is for the institution to have a competent landscape architectural firm to work with the institution on a continuing basis.

It is so easy for the institution to choose the local landscape architect for the job. Or, especially in state institutions, it is the line of least resistance to appoint a landscape architect from within the state. Certainly, both of these could be the best in the country and deserve the appointment. However, most likely they are not. In any case they should be considered in making the selection. The selection should be on a national basis and even international if the cost of travel is not prohibitive.

The landscape architectural firm serves as an effective scapegoat for the institution's administrator and board of control when alumni/ae and local faculty members, and local citizens and legislatures and whatnot put pressure on the administration to tear down or let remain a certain building, or place a new building in a certain place or cut down all of the trees or not dare cut down a tree.

Consistency in campus architectural design or style seems to be an impossible thing in this country. Some colleges and universities have made a conscious effort to keep the same type of exteriors of buildings throughout the campus but few have done so. It can be done when there is enough money available to build a completely new campus in another location, but if the institution grows and needs other buildings, the chances are that the type of architecture adopted will change. Even the colleges and the universities with the most money have made a dramatic departure from the style of their older buildings. One reason for this departure is that Gothic buildings made out of stone, for instance, are extremely expensive. Some say that the function required of some buildings do not lend themselves to certain types of architecture, but this is questionable. Possibly the most potent reason for the departure is that there are a lot of hard-headed architects and a lot of soft-headed presidents of colleges and universities. Most architects make up their minds what a building that they are designing should look like on the exterior and seem to have an extraordinary capacity to demonstrate their tenacity or bullheadedness. This seems to be a part of the breed. Often all of this comes to the surface after the contract is given to a certain architect. Then the president or some of his assistants have the problem of talking the architect into something else, or changing architects which is costly and sometimes politically impossible.

This brings us full-scale into the problem of choosing architects. In some instances the governor of the state chooses the architects for state buildings, including the buildings on the campuses of state-supported colleges and universities. Often he does it on the basis of the architects in the state who supported (gave money to) his campaign. Often it is done by giving the designing job for the first state building in the governor's tenure to the architectural firm that contributed the largest amount of money to his campaign and right on down the pecking scale.

Sometimes persuasion is effective from the institution to the governor or from the board of control to the governor. But usually the one wanted must have been on the list of the governor's financial backers.

Some governors do not pay any attention to the choice of architects and then the board of control usually makes the decision after the institution makes recommendations. There is no assurance that an institution will get one of the best architects when the board of control makes the choice because usually boards of state-supported institutions are made up of small-time politicians who act that way on occasions. These people--most of them--were appointed to the board by the governor in payment for their support in helping him get elected.

I recall one time when I got an alumna to give her alma mater enough money to build a chapel for the university. We conducted an international competition for an architect. An architect from St. Louis, Missouri, won it. As in all cases of getting architects for building my recommendation had to go to the board of trustees for approval. My recommendation went to the building committee of the board of trustees. Before that group I explained how we conducted the international competition and how pleased we were to recommend the man from St. Louis to be the architect. Immediately after my presentation a member of the committee spoke up and said an architect from within the state just completed a church in his hometown, and he did such a fine job of it that this architect should be given the job under consideration. Other discussion concerning the project followed. I was sitting by the chairman of the committee. He leaned over to me and whispered: "Did the donor request an architect?" I got the message. The donor had not requested an architect. I asked for the floor and requested that my request for the architect be tabled until the next meeting and in the meantime I would look into the qualifications of the person who was the architect for the church in my good friend's hometown. The committee tabled the motion until the next meeting. After I returned to my office I put in a call for the donor. Her secretary answered and told me the donor would not be available until the next morning. I asked the secretary if she would be so kind as to relay to the donor the details of what had happened at the committee meeting concerning the naming of an architect for the chapel. She agreed and I gave her the story. She told me the donor would call me the next morning at ten o'clock. Sure enough the next morning at ten o'clock my telephone was ringing and my executive secretary told me that the donor wanted to speak to me. I picked up the telephone and the donor said that she wanted to make a request. I agreed and she said: "I request that the architect from St. Louis be the architect for the chapel." I swallowed once or twice and said: "I'll be very glad to relay that to the board of trustees." With that she said: "You can also tell the board of trustees that if they do not name the architect from St. Louis as the architect, I withdraw my gift to finance the building of the chapel." "Yes, yes," was my answer. I thanked the lady who, until her secretary gave her my message, had never heard of the architect from St. Louis. At the next meeting of the board of trustees--approximately one month later--I relayed both of the donor's statements to the building committee and the committee recommended that the architect from St. Louis be the architect and the board approved the recommendation unanimously. He drew up the plans and supervised the construction of a chapel that, when it was finished, was a gem and was approved by the donor, the board of trustees, and almost all who have seen or worshipped in it.

111

Naming contractors is equally as frustrating as naming architects. Naming contractors appears to be a very simple undertaking. All you have to do is to call for bids and give the contract to the best bidder. Once in awhile it is that simple, but usually it is not. The reason why it is not is because it is difficult to determine which bid is the best. The best usually is defined as the lowest by a qualified contractor. It takes very few brains to figure out which one is the lowest, but to determine which contractors are qualified is the problem. Some contractors have their attorneys to attend bid openings. If a given contractor has the low bid, he and his lawyer have to try to convince everyone that he is qualified to do the job. If he is not the low bidder, often he and his lawyer go after the low bidder to prove that he is not qualified.

Usually contractors are extremely competitive, but occasionally they resort to collusion. It happened when I was in the process of getting a new home for the president.

Most presidents of universities prefer to live in substandard quarters rather than try to get a new home for the president. The reasons are twofold: one is that the tenure of a president is very short; and secondly, to get a new home is a tricky undertaking in that the result seems to displease most of the people.

When I was president of a certain university my board of trustees expressed interest in my having a better place in which to live in than the president's home in which I was living had served all of the presidents of that institution and was pretty well worn out. I told the board I would agree if they would decide how much should be put into it, and would get the legislature to put up the entire amount. The board determined the amount and the legislature passed a bill providing the entire amount. My recommendation of an architect was approved all the way through and he drew up the plans that were approved by my wife and myself and the board of trustees. We advertised for bids and only one bid was submitted, and it was for an amount that far exceeded the amount that the legislature had made available. The architect was stunned because he thought his specifications were within the money. The one bid was rejected and we called for bids on another date. Upon investigation we found that the one contractor who submitted a bid went to all of the other contractors who were working to place a bid and talked them into letting him have the contract. It was easy for him to find out which other contractors were planning to bid on it because they have to get copies of the specifications from the architect, and it is not difficult to find out which contractors got them from someone in the architect's office. In this instance only four others got them. Just how this one contractor got the others not to submit a bid we did not try to determine. Anyway, this collusion put us to work. We went to other contracts and talked three others into submitting bids at the second bid opening. One of them was within the money and from a qualified contractor, so he got the job. He built the house within the money and to our satisfaction. The house did not satisfy everyone, but it was better than what we had and it will serve satisfactorily for some time to come.

Getting contractors to build in keeping with the specifications is another sticky problem. This is the job of the architect, but most architects do not provide enough supervision to assure that the building is being constructed in keeping with the specifications. It is difficult to understand why this is true. Of course, supervision costs money and most architects are as close with their money as they are detailed in their plans. However, one architect gave a university where I was the president enough money to construct a small building on the river primarily for the recreation of the president and his family.

The college or university should have a person with architectural or contracting experience on the institution staff or on the staff at the board of control office to check on the architects and contractors to see that they do their work in keeping with the specifications. Lawsuits can be the result, and sometimes the job has to be changed over from one contractor to another. All of this is costly, but overall it usually costs less because the building will be constructed in keeping with the specifications. Cutting corners to make money will be eliminated.

Renovation is about as expensive as new construction. Sometimes it is more expensive, and when the effort gets into the category of repairs, it is less expensive.

Demolition at one time could be done for the price of the materials. It, like removing a tree, has escalated in price almost beyond comprehension.

When repairing will not do the job and state law or local interests, etc., will not permit demolition, the only recourse is renovation. The procedure for this is the same as for the construction of a new building.

To have a competent superintendent of grounds and buildings is important. Under him will be specialists in electricity, plumbing, construction, cleaning, gardening, air conditioning and heating, etc.

These maintenance people should have a systematic schedule of inspection. Such supervision and repair, such as in air conditioning, can save a considerable amount of money.

The people who work on the upkeep of the grounds will do their work in keeping with the landscape architect's plan for the campus.

Plumbers can save large amounts of money by periodically checking all plumbing to repair leaks.

Safety and proper wattage for the use of the eyes are the responsibilities of electricians.

Utility bills have skyrocketed and entirely too much money is now going in that direction, compared with the amount going into teacher's salaries.

Some maintenance shops are unionized, but most of them are not. Unions usually become interested when special projects are undertaken. For instance, the painters' union will move in sometimes to declare a closed shop on repainting a number of buildings. Usually a closed shop can be avoided, if such is desired, by paying union wages to both the union members and the nonunion people on the job.

To have a physical plant that operates smoothly is an art and almost a miracle.

Many people can get tremendously upset by any little thing that goes wrong in a building. They should be permitted to report emergencies to the maintenance department by telephone. All other requests should be reported in writing by campus mail. The definition of "an emergency" should be in writing and in the hands of all who would make requests for repairs. Many can be made happy by expeditious handling of repair requests.

Pilfering is a problem in maintenance departments. This is done by employees within the department or others employed by the institution who have access to supplies. Constant supervision not by one person because he might be the one who is doing the stealing, but by his supervisors is the best way in which to cut down or eliminate pilfering.

Pilfering is not confined to maintenance departments. It can go anywhere in the university. That is the reason why it is so very important to keep up-to-date an inventory control of every item in the university. An inventory control is expensive, but in the long run, it saves money.

Burglary is possible anywhere at any time. It is done at colleges and universities, in some cases by insiders and in other cases by outsiders. In any case it is a matter for law enforcement officers. When caught they should be punished if proven guilty, and if they are university employees, they should be dismissed and never reemployed by that university.

It should be noted that some of the men and women working in the institution's maintenance department, cafeterias, laundry, infirmary, etc., have been with the institution for many years and are extremely loyal to the university. Some of these people are "favorites" with the students and faculty. They are true assets for the institution. They are good public relations people for the college or university. The quality controls for buildings and grounds are the licensing of the architects, inspection by board of control staff members, and the institution's administrators.

Alumni/ae

Alumni and alumnae and alumnus and alumna will be referred to in this writing in a way that is unusual. Alumnae will refer to the plural of both men and women, and alumnu will refer to the singular of both women and men.

It is extremely important for every college and university to have an alumnae association.

An alumnae association has a constitution and bylaws. The constitution permits the organization to raise money, have a program in the interest of the university, and operate as a tax-exempt entity. The bylaws are usually easy to change and makes it possible for those in charge to meet changing needs.

The association has an executive director who is a full-time employed person who is an alumnu of the institution. Usually the association has a staff large enough to take care of the association's business, but in some instances there is not enough money available to provide for such.

The association has elected officers to serve specified periods of time and a board of directors who have staggered terms in order to provide continuity to the work of the association.

The executive director reports to the president of the association and to the president of the institution. Often the report to the president of the institution is through someone else at a lower level such as vice-president for external affairs.

The financing of the operation comes from dues, annual contributions, special endowment funds, special projects, operation of special programs or services for the institution, special terminal projects, and from the institution's budget. Usually the institution's budget has a line item in it for the association that makes up the difference between the amount of income that the association is able to generate and what it takes to pay expenses for the year. Often this is a bone of contention in that the association executives or leaders want more from the institution in order to launch a larger program or have a larger or more expensive staff. The institution would prefer for the association's program to be cost-effective but seldom is it in such a condition. However, institutional administrators are often hard pressed by alumnae, trustees and/or alumnae visiting committees to allocate as much as possible to alumnae association work.

The alumnae association staff performs a number of duties. It sounds relatively simply but a very difficult task of the staff is to keep the alumnae records up-to-date. The records can be very comprehensive including much information about each alumnu, or they can record only the name, address, and class of each alumnu. Even the latter is almost exasperating because there are seemingly endless changed taking place. However, this is the least that an institution should do for a graduate; and of course, it is the source of what the graduate or alumnu who attended but did not graduate can do for the institution.

The one publication that requires the most time of the staff members is the Alumnae Magazine. This magazine, when well done, means more to the alumnae than practically any other magazine that they receive.

There should be someone on the alumnae association staff who knows something about journalism in order to let that knowledge reflect in the quality of the Alumnae Magazine. The item in these magazines that is of greatest interest to alumnae is the activities of their classmates and of the other students who they knew in college. Many of these alumnae do not get back to the campus for reunions and the best way in which they can get information about their college acquaintances is through the Alumnae Magazine.

A major emphasis in Alumnae Magazines is to keep alumnae up-to-date on happenings at the institution. Every issue of the magazine should include such information. This should not only include the gist of what has happened, but also an outline of what the administrators and board members would like to see happen at the institution. The latter is a way in which the institution can get alumnae support for its program.

Some alumnae associations send to alumnae some special reports and newsletters. These are necessary in order to get across to the alumnae the reasons for and the implications of special items that are of great interest to the institution.

Alumnae homecomings are arranged by the alumnae staff and officers with the cooperation of institution officers. These annual events honor the classes of certain years. An effort is made to get all of the living graduates of these classes to return to the campus for the festivities. Many alumnae make special efforts to attend these reunions.

Homecomings are more than the gathering of certain classes for reunion. All alumnae are invited and urged to attend. They are members of the association and a business session of the association is held at each homecoming. Here the financial reports are presented and the program for the future is discussed and acted upon. Usually the homecoming includes a speech or a report to the alumnae by the president of the institution. This is a great opportunity for the president to tell the alumnae what he expects for the institution and how they--the alumnae--can help achieve these objectives.

Many of these homecomings honor the outstanding achievements of alumnae. Some receive certificates and others receive pins. Some receive resolutions and others listen to words of commendation. The selection of those to receive such recognition is difficult and should be done by a committee because one person might not be able to withstand the pressure from those who thought they should have been included but were not. Some institutions have discontinued or not started such recognitions because they were of the opinion that they did more harm than good.

Most homecomings have some sort of entertainment. Often the homecomings are arranged around football games. Others have concerts. Usually alumnae prefer to listen to students rather than to hear professionals.

Alumnae association staff members arrange many special events such as Founders' Day programs. These require considerable planning time, but are vital in the life of the institution.

All alumnae associations should conduct training programs for volunteer alumnae to do specific jobs. A pathetic phenomenon is an alumnu who tries to do something for the alma mater but is not well informed. These people can represent the institution to others as it was when they were enrolled and not as it is now or would like to be in the future. Thus the purposes of the training programs are to get the volunteers up-to-date in regard to the institution and give them specifics in regard to the project that they are to promote.

Alumnae associations arrange cruises and special trips for alumnae who are interested and can afford to pay for them. All of these pay for themselves and offer an opportunity for good fellowship and continuing interest in the institution. Some of these cruises also offer courses en route and give credit for such. This comes under the general heading of continuing education.

117

Continuing education projects promoted by alumnae associations are numerous. Some give credit and others are of a noncredit nature. Alumnae colleges are held on weekends at some institutions. These give little credit, but they give an opportunity for alumnae to update themselves in their greatest interests. Conferences and one-day seminars are held for alumnae. On-campus and off-campus lecture series are held for alumnae. Reading lists prepared by members of the faculty are made available to alumnae through the alumnae office. Some colleges and universities cooperate with other colleges and universities in providing continuing education for alumnae.

Alumnae associations have alumnae clubs. An alumnae club is any group of alumnae of any given institution anywhere who decide that they want to meet periodically and get permission from the alumnae association to do so. Some of them have constitutions and bylaws, but most of them elect officers and go from there. These clubs provide good fellowship and a continuing contact with the alma mater. Some clubs are formed in other countries and rather than having a national alumnae association, it is international. Many college and university presidents visit alumnae clubs not only to make speeches at the clubs, but also to make contacts with people in the area where the club is located. Often alumnae introduce the president to people who can give much support to the institution. These clubs can be of influence in getting capable students from the area to attend their alma mater.

Alumnae are to an institution of higher learning as stockholders are to a corporation. They paid money to get their college education and many of them contribute money each year to the alumnae fund. They can vote on issues concerning the institution at each annual meeting of the alumnae association. They can write to the president of the institution or go to see him at any time. They may express their views and wishes for the institution and most institutional administrators appreciate such interest and support.

Alumnae can be a nuisance. For instance, they can want the institution to be exactly as it was when they were college students even if they finished thirty years ago. No one can turn back the hands of time and not many want to do so. Even if they could, and recapture some of the good things of the past that have been lost, rarely would such fit the needs and desires of present-day students.

Some people say that alumnae are more interested in their alma mater having a winning football team than anything else. This is simply not true. Of course, they are interested in having a winning football team, but they are also interested in their institution winning in all of the other enterprises that it undertakes. The college spirit is not out of all of them yet and they want to whoop and holler once in awhile. It is better for the institution for them to do such at a football game than at a meeting of the board of control. However, often they do it at both!

Private institutions more than the state-supported institutions depend heavily on the financial contributions of alumnae. The way in which to get the money is to keep the alumnae fully informed and excited about the well-being of their alma mater.

Alumnae should be represented on the board of control and on visiting committees of the institution. They should be represented on important institutional committees such as those having to do with planning and development.

Every senior college and university has a foundation and this is run primarily by the alumnae.

Some alumnae are interested in perpetuating the names of some of their favorite professors. They do this by establishing scholarships in their honor and this money is used to help needy and worthy students attend the college. This sort of thing helps to get enrollment in a significant way.

At the other end of the scale, alumnae can help students and their alma mater by assisting the institution's placement bureau in getting jobs for graduates. Colleges and universities should do more than they do to help graduates get not only their initial jobs, but also jobs throughout their lives. Alumnae have jobs to fill, and they can be very influential with their friends in getting jobs for graduates of their alma mater. A person never forgets anyone who helps him get a good job or a promotion.

Alumnae essential? Obviously, yes. The effectiveness of an institution of higher learning can be judged by the records made by its alumnae. Loyalty to alma mater is another index of the institution's effectiveness. Some would say that the best index of effectiveness is the amount of money that the alumnae give to their alma mater; however, earning money is only one aspect of success and of what higher education expects it's graduates to do.

An individual does not have to have a college degree to be considered an alumni of an institution, but he must have had to be enrolled there. Those who administer and teach at the institution should always remember that there is nothing better than a satisfied customer.

The Executive Secretary of the Alumnae Association and the Director of Development should work together to keep the alumnae up-to-date about accomplishments and needs of the institution.

These people should have manuals of operation that will help them keep the quality of their work at a high level. Both of them are responsible to higher administrative officers and the happiness of the alumnae and the amount of money raised from the alumnae and others are the factors that determine their effectiveness.

Public Relations

A product achieves its potential only when it is merchandized properly. This statement truly applies to higher education as much as it does to soap, toothpaste, tobacco, or anything else that people can get along somehow with or without. In other words, higher education is partially a selling game. It can continue to survive somehow in some cases without it, but it cannot reach its highest potential without it.

Selling is a word that educators in general dislike. They think it is not appropriate when applied to higher education. They think the public should recognize the value of higher education without any promotion. Many people do not even like to use the word "merchandizing" when referring to higher education. Therefore, they use the title "public relations." This often boils down to "public information" or telling it like it is.

All of it starts with the head of the institution, but goes much beyond him because his tenure is short and the institution "must go on." If the president is not an effective public relations person, he is in the wrong job. Some presidents are "low-key," some are "pistol-balls," and most of the others are in-between. A president cannot remain in his job if he is so "low-key" that he cannot be respected and even admired by some group, such as the alumni, the faculty, the students, the public, etc. On the other hand, he cannot remain in his job if he is so much of a pistal-ball that he alienates all or many groups. The more groups he can have respect and admire him, the longer he can stay on the job.

In any cases, the head of the institution sets the tone of the institution. He should clearly declare that he is counting on every student, every faculty member, every administrator, and every staff member to exert a positive influence toward the institution. They are not expected to take the place of the public relations officers of the institution, but they should realize that their actions and comments reflect either favorably or unfavorably upon the institution, and as long as they choose to work there, they should see that their actions reflect favorably upon the institution. This point of view is not welcomed by some of the people who are on the payrolls of colleges and universities, but these people should realize that higher education is not what it used to be. It is now highly competitive and needs to reestablish the value of higher education in the minds of prospective students and the public.

Two words used in the preceding sentence represent the basic goals of a public relations department in an institution of higher learning. The words are "competition" and "value."

The public relations department of an institution of higher learning should work out a plan for that institution to compete successfully in getting students to enroll at that institution rather than at other institutions. Also, it should include in the plan demonstrations of the value of higher education at that institution.

The answer to this is to find the uniqueness of that institution and tie it to the needs of the people. What is it that this institution offers that no other institution offers? Why should a student enroll at this institution rather than at another one? Why should a faculty member elsewhere want to join this faculty? Why should others (the legislature, the church, foundations, individuals, etc.) want to give money to this institution? Research to answer questions like these should be conducted year-round.

Not many people can be forced to do very much. The objective is to get them to want to do it. People get to want something through their senses. Let them see it, hear it, smell it, or taste it, and they might want it. Public relations people should get the facts as mentioned in the paragraph above and package them in such a way that people see or hear these things about the university and will want to enroll or support it.

This can be done through the media, by mail, or in person. Actually all three are required to get the job done effectively.

Anything that happens at the institution will be known--maybe not by many but by some, and maybe not now but later. It is wise to function on the theory that if you do not want it known, you had better not do it. There is no such thing as a complete cover-up when people are involved. Someone will hear, see, or tell it. If it is bad news, the news media will find it. Sometimes the news media is interested in good news, but rarely does such cross a state border. Some news reporters do not want to work through public relations departments. They think the news is slanted and so it is--in the interest of the institution. It is important for the public relations department to beat the news reporter to the punch because often when the outside reporter goes to the source on the campus, he uncovers other things that are not very complimentary and often makes a mountain out of a mole hill. So let the event be known in the best light possible, and of course without distorting the facts.

Truthfulness must be the foundation on which all promotion efforts for the institution are based. To send a brochure in color through the mail to prospective students claiming a swimming pool at each dormitory when in fact there is not such can get the institution in trouble, not only with the public, but also with the accrediting agencies. Mail literature promoting colleges and universities has become very creative and effective.

There is nothing more effective in promoting colleges and universities than having attractive and intelligent and sincere people making presentations to visitors on the campus or to groups and individuals in the area from which the institution draws or would like to draw students or support. All forms of visual aids are used at such sessions and they are effective. Public Relations offices should have a first-class speakers' bureau through which speakers from the institution can be obtained by interested groups.

Regular radio and television programs using student talent have been effective in getting a following.

Facts and figures and charts are used to get a following at church conferences, legislative committee meetings, and even before boards of control.

Automobile stickers, pennants, caps, sweaters, automobile plates, and other items have been used effectively in keeping the name of the institution before the public.

Yes, public relations is salesmanship, but it is more than that. It is also high-quality journalism and photography.

Every public relations staff must have on it people who are talented and educated and experienced in many types of writing. These people must be able to write newspaper articles, radio script, television script, brochure script, and speeches. More than that some of the people must be sportswriters. These people must not only be able to write well, they should know the people for whom they are writing and send them the type of articles that they will print. Time is wasted when an editor gets an article that he will not print. However, public relations or information people must take chances on getting their materials printed because the type of article that will not get printed one time might get printed the next time. Editors have their good days and their bad days. They have their prejudices although they would not admit it. They have more news than they can print at one time, and will need fillers at another time. It is important for the director of public information to work with the public information news writer—especially the new ones—and keep them from getting so disappointed when so many of their articles do not get printed that they will want to give up and quit the job. It is desirable for every public relations office to have a contract or agreement with a clipping service so that charts may be made of printed stories compared with the number and type of stories sent out. This gives direction to further writing which gets better results.

Some people who are not acquainted with college public relations work are of the opinion that those who work in such an office would not have much to write about. This is not correct. Just as the sportswriter has every game to write up, a news writer in the public information office has everyone in the institution to write about. If the news writer were to write an article about all of the achievements of the faculty members and the students, it would flood the media in a way that it had never seen, even during a political election. Every public information officer should work out appropriate methods of getting people to report such achievements to them and then follow up with interviews.

The Chinese proverb saying that a picture is worth a thousand words is still true. Excellent photographers must be employed as members of the public information staff. They must be able to show up anywhere at any time, take a good picture, get the facts about it, or at least enough for another member of the staff to go to the source and get enough facts to write the story and then rush to his darkroom at the public information office and develop the negative and have the picture ready to send out at once.

The same kind of pictures that will be used by the media are not always the kind that are needed for brochures. Some photographers on the public information staff should be able to take pictures for brochures, because brochures are extremely effective in promotion. They should be placed in many different types of places. The writer and his wife attend an international home show last week and the local junior college maintained a booth there and gave out beautiful and very effective brochures about the college.

Through pictures much can be accomplished. When the writer was president of a junior college, he got Life magazine to send a photographer and a writer to the college to prepare a story about the college for the magazine. They sent a world-famous photographer and a writer from the Time staff to do the job. The photographer took about a thousand pictures at the college and the writer gathered all of the facts that he desired. They were on the campus doing their work for about a week. A write-up of the type of college that it was, illustrated by many pictures in color, covered six pages of one issue of Life magazine. This did not cost the college anything and it created considerable interest in the college throughout the nation.

Some colleges and universities arrive at the conclusion that they need help in promoting their institutions and they call in promotion agencies from outside. These people are expensive because some of them have been successful in promoting candidates for governorships and seats in the U.S. Senate. The writer called in such an agency that had recently handled the publicity to elect the governors of two nearby states. It was a fascinating experience because they could see the university as those of us who worked there could not. Also they knew how to state things in a way that the general public could understand and remember. The drawback was that not any of them had ever promoted a university and they knew nothing about doing so. Nevertheless those of us at the university gained some new insights from the experience and told them that if we ever decided to run for a governorship, we would call on them again.

Full returns from the efforts of higher education will not be realized if the public does not know about what it has to offer and what it has accomplished. To get this information across to the public is an essential for each and every college and university.

Quality controls in public relations must result in truthfulness, caring for people, love for the institution, effectiveness as a writer or speaker or photographer, being up-to-date on what is happening at the institution, initiative and diplomacy.

Incentives like compliments, better working conditions, raises in salary and high quality work at the institution spur people on. Such is needed to get the public to react favorably when the name of the institution is mentioned, and for them to care about the institution and want to help to make it even better.

Standards

Standards come from almost everywhere and they are checked periodically for adequacy by accrediting agencies. The accrediting agencies will not let them get too low, and the institutions can place them as high as they desire.

Faculty members have a large input in regard to scholastic standards. This means that if the standards for the employment and retention of faculty members are not high, there is little hope of having high scholastic standards for student performance. Highly qualified faculty members want the institution to admit only highly qualified students. The reason for this is that they are easier to teach and they have greater promise of learning more.

The standard that receives the greatest amount of attention

124

is the entrance standard. Athletic departments are vitally interested in this because it has a great deal to do with the success of their recruiting efforts. Some athletic departments stand for high entrance standards, but most of them want them to be as low as possible. The people in this latter category will settle for the minimum standards as set by the athletic conferences. Some institutions are independents as far as athletic association is concerned and without having to meet conference entrance standards, some of them put on the pressure for the institution to accept for entrance almost anyone with great athletic potential.

A few athletic departments and their alumni will misrepresent scholastic records and examination to get choice prospects accepted for entrance. Some of these are caught in the process and are punished by the institution, the conference and/or NCAA.

Alumni/ae are interested in entrance standards for several reasons. Some as stated above want to get choice athletes into the institution. They prefer the ones who have great athletic ability and who are able on their own to meet the scholastic requirements. Many alumni and alumnae want their children to enter and graduate from their alma maters. Generally speaking, the entrance standards have gone up since they entered college and if they had been so high then as they are now, many of them would not have made it! Anyway these people want the entrance standard set where their children can get in and some of them have inherited a bit from their fathers and mothers. Many alumni/ae like to know or brag about their alma maters being institutions of high standing. This they think makes them look better. Therefore, there is input and pressure from the alumni for the setting of certain entrance standards.

Often legislatures and church conferences are interested in entrance requirements. Such usually comes when they are looking for ways and means of supplying less money or at least not any additional money to the institutions. It is interesting how scholarly a nonscholarly member of the legislature or church conference can talk when he is advocating higher entrance standards. You would think he is trying to get a place in The International Who's Who of Intellectuals!

Members of the present-day student body are interested in entrance standards. If they are lowered it cheapens their standing, not only in their own eyes, but also in the eyes of their acquaintances. If they are raised, the student is wondering if the standards to remain enrolled in the institution might be raised and, if so, whether he can make it.

A very practical question that faces administrators and boards of control has to do with money. Do we have enough students enrolled to fill the dormitories? Are we getting enough money from student tuition when put with our other income to come out in the black?

Taking all of these points and others into consideration, institutional administrators have to come up with an entrance standard that meets accrediting-agency requirements and meets the needs of the institution. Some few institutions cannot even meet the requirements of the accrediting agencies in this respect and they have to operate without accreditation or close down. The president of the institution recommends the entrance standard to the board of control and it is approved or amended and remains in operation until the board approves a change.

Many or most institutions take the easy way out in regard to an entrance standard. They accept or reject students based on one score on one test. This really is not necessarily a fair determination of a person's ability to meet college requirements for a degree. No test that humans have devised is capable of doing this. College entrance should be based on a regression equation worked out for each college as stated above.

Now we must give consideration to the standards for students to remain enrolled in college. What scholastic average must a student have at the end of every term to remain enrolled in a given institution? Should students who do not do well scholastically be placed on scholastic probation for a specified period of time before being dropped? When should a student be dismissed for scholastic reasons? Should a student who has been dropped be readmitted and, if so, under what conditions?

Even a regression equation for entrance does not guarantee what a student will do in his scholastic work in college. It predicts rather accurately what a student is capable of doing. However, college students are young and still in the process of growing up, and some of them will lose interest for one reason or another. The purpose of having scholastic performance standards for retention in college is twofold. In the first place, there is little sense in wasting the student's time and his or his parents' money in retaining him if he does not show promise of meeting graduation requirements. Of course, just a little of it is good for him, but often it falls into the category of "a little knowledge is a dangerous thing." The other reason is that a teacher can more profitably use his time teaching students who want to learn.

Yes, all students should be required to maintain a certain average in order to remain enrolled. Warning should be given in the form of scholastic probation for one term prior to dismissal. Any student who has been dismissed for not maintaining a high enough scholastic average should have the privilege of reenrolling one more time after a year has elapsed.

Naturally, there must be certain standards set for degrees. Usually they are to complete a certain pattern of courses--some required, some recommended, and some free choices--a specified number of credit hours of work, and achieve a certain average. Many institutions have other requirements.

In most of the institutions of higher learning, scholastic standards are acted upon by the faculty senate. Every faculty senate, administration, and board of control should do everything in their power to keep or get scholastic standards at the institution to be as high as the intellectual ability and educational background of the students, and the financial resources of the institution will permit.

Unfortunately this means that degrees are not the same. Any degree from any institution of higher learning is not necessarily the same as the same degree from another college or university. More than that, a degree from any given college or university may not be of the same quality as the same degree from that institution at an earlier or later date. The quality of a degree from any college or university depends upon the standards that were in force at that institution at the time that the student was enrolled. And the standards in force at that time depended upon the quality of instruction that the institution could afford and attract, and the vigor that was exerted in upholding and improving standards.

Another type of standard has to do with student conduct.

The tremendous growth of some institutions brought with it a depersonalization trend and some of them are not very much unlike factories in that students check in and out in somewhat the same manner as laborers do on a punch-card system. Most of these students do not live on campus and they may do as they wish without any supervision by the institution of higher learning.

The student uprising of the sixties brought a new freedom to students. Due process laws, for instance, gave a new slant to the supervision of students who live in dormitories, as well as to all students in the classroom.

Nevertheless, some colleges and not many universities still try to control or shape the actions of students while they are on campus. The use of alcohol, the use of narcotics, destroying institution property, stealing, cheating, rape, physical violence, closing hours for dormitories, visiting hours in dormitories, and the like are usually dealt with by student senates, with the assistance of faculty or administration advisers. Some of these situations are turned over to the city police department.

127

Cheating in classroom work and class attendance is usually dealt with by the teacher of the class where it takes place.

The guiding principle in student campus conduct is for the student not to hurt himself and not to interfere with the rights of others. The interpretation placed on this principle varies with the size and type of institution involved and the mores of the community in which the institution is located.

In any college or university, as in any other group of humans, there are some people who will let the end justify the means. These people can cause no need of trouble when it comes to living in keeping with standards. Here we have one of the most exasperating problems of administration. Most of these problems have to do with students wanting to be admitted to college and not having the qualifications to meet entrance requirements, wanting to remain enrolled after being dismissed, and students wanting a degree but not quite meeting the requirements.

Parents of students who have been dismissed have appealed to all of the appeal boards within the institution, the board of control, the governor of the state, the legislature, and to members of Congress. Parents of students who did not quite meet graduation requirements have offered deans large amounts of money to change the record in such a way that their offspring could graduate on time or as scheduled. Department heads and deans have been known to overlook specific course requirements when they did not have authority to do so. Presidents of colleges and universities have been known to admit students who did not meet entrance requirements. Members of boards of control, members of legislatures, and governors have been known to make requests and put pressure on institutional administrators to do things that were not in keeping with established standards and policies. Such actions are the exceptions, but those who hold responsible positions in colleges and universities must be ready to deal with them when they occur and politely refuse to comply. This will bring consternation for awhile but over the long run it will bring respect. It is great to be loved and to have many friends, but in one's professional work it is far more important to be respected. Without respect, a person cannot be an effective leader for very long. Possibly one reason why the tenure of college and university presidents on the average is so short is because they do not give enough attention to improving and upholding standards.

Standards are essential in higher education. Without enforcement of high standards high quality education is impossible.

Quality control is intermingled in all of higher education. It serves the purpose of seeing that performance is in keeping with standards. The question for the people in any college or university is to determine if their standards are high enough to assure students an education of high quality. The faculty and administrators can get assistance on this question from their reading of professional journals and from their conversations with colleagues at national meetings. Also, they can receive help from accrediting agencies. If the standards are found to need adjusting, the faculty and the administrators can modify them accordingly.

There should be a manual for very department in the university telling what is expected of those who work in the department. These guidelines should be designed to enhance the quality of the work to be done.

Worth

No attempt will be made to list all of the reasons why a college education is valuable, but many of them will be listed.

The better jobs with higher paying salaries go to college graduates. This should be viewed from the time a person is twenty-two years of age until he quits work. Some people without college degrees get more money than college graduates in the beginning, but soon they hit a plateau and from there on it is extremely difficult for them to get higher. Whereas, a college graduate is more likely to get the job in the beginning and after he gets it his responsibilities usually increase and he is more apt to be promoted and receive higher pay. This has been traditionally true for men, and it is doubly true for women who are now holding jobs in ever-increasing numbers. For women to get top responsible jobs is still very difficult, and without at least a bachelor's degree, it is the exception and not the rule. Many college graduates are now staying on for a master's degree--which usually requires only one more year of work--before getting a job so that they can be just one jump ahead of most of the others. It is wise to do so especially for women because no man will willingly give his good job over to anyone, especially a woman! It is my belief that the battle of the future in the gender revolution will be at the point of women taking over top or near-top jobs from men. Competence will win but only after a bitter struggle, which it is hoped will not leave the institution known as the family in shambles. Women will continue to flood the job market until husbands can earn enough to support the family. After that takes place, divorce rates will begin to subside. Then after that, many women will remain in the world of work outside the home, but the number will be fewer and the hectic competition will subside somewhat.

After getting a job, or in many cases before getting a job, people are thinking about getting married. College is not supposed to be a matrimonial bureau, but many people marry people whom they met in college. A value that going to college offers is a wider range of acquaintances from which a person can choose a mate. One university official said that ninety percent of the young women who enrolled in the institution with which he was connected did so with the primary objective of meeting, falling in love with, and marrying a man who would be in one of the professions. Evidently that person was not aware of the burning desire that women have for a college education so that they can make it on their own if they choose to do so or if they have to do so. The notion seems to be around today that women are doing all of the chasing. It appears that men have not given any ground in this respect. The liberation of women has just given women the opportunity to catch up with the men in this respect. The chase continues. A college campus is an ideal setting for the chase. Right on!

Many people are of the opinion that young people are interested only in temporary pleasures and things. This, of course, is true with some young people but many of them are looking for permanent things. Things that they can have forever. Things that no one can take away from them. A college education is something that no one can take away from anyone. With crime on the increase almost anyone can be mugged, robbed, or raped at any time. As awful as that is, whoever did it could not take away the victim's college education. A person can incapacitate another, but still he cannot take away his college education. It is permanent for as long as the person lives. Most of what a person get in an undergraduate education is an introduction or beginning of higher things. It grows with use, like in the appreciation of good literature. Some of it becomes outdated and should be brought up-to-date through private study or formal classes. But it is good for a person's entire life, and such permanency is appreciated by many people.

Two years of college is enough for many people. The tremendous growth of junior colleges and their enrollment has been almost a phenomenon in this country. Some of their work is preparation for senior college entrance, but most of it is in vocational and technical work. The value of this type of college work has been indispensable to industry in our nation. These associate-degree graduates are able to get into a trade quickly and make a living, and this is important in our society.

Specialization at the four-year level is becoming increasingly popular. Most of these people want to learn how to do what they will be expected to do on a job. For instance, a person wants to design houses so he majors in architecture. A college education is valuable because it teaches a person how to do this. But a college education amounts to more than teaching a person how to design houses. The basic part of a college education is general education. The would-be architect must

130

complete a core curriculum which is designed to make him knowledgeable in the humanities, natural sciences, and physical sciences.

Another value of college is the opportunity for a person to get a liberal education. Any student can get this if he tries even if he has chosen to major in architecture or any other highly specialized field. He is more apt to get it if he majors in the humanities, natural sciences, or physical sciences because here he can spend less time on specialization and more time on a broader range of subjects.

A student in college has the opportunity to search for the truth. He has heard many things and he has talked with people who have held many opinions. Usually they conflict. Which ones are correct? A college student soon finds that truth can be obtained by scientific experimentation or by philosophical analysis. There is no end to how much exploration he can undertake.

A college student cannot avoid getting some knowledge. How much he gets depends to a great extent upon his own inquisitiveness. He soon finds that to merely memorize is not enough. He needs to think about it, figure out what it means, and reflect on its possible application.

Some college students are interested in acquiring wisdom. These people soon find that it is based on knowledge. Knowledge within itself is worthy, but it meets its fullest fruition when it is put into use. Wisdom is how to make the best choices from that knowledge. Then to act wisely is the greatest achievement that humans can attain.

Students in college have an opportunity to develop a philosophy of life. All people have some sort of a philosophy of life whether it is formulated or not and whether or not it appears that they act in keeping with it. During college is a good time to formulate one even though it will be revised time and time again as the individual receives additional knowledge and insight.

Some colleges, especially those that are church related, are very much interested in having students grown religiously while they are in college. College students have such an opportunity through courses in religion, and participation in religious associations, etc. Such is also available in independent and state-supported colleges.

To have a reservoir of knowledge, understanding, and appreciation is an asset that many people would like to possess. To know good music, to appreciate good paintings, to enjoy good literature, these are the types of things in the reservoir and no college student is without some of it.

To have confidence in one's ability to face any new situation unafraid with the ability to think about it and reason one's way through it is a part of what a student can get in college.

With such equipment as stated above it would be difficult to imagine how such a person could avoid being a responsible citizen. Our democracy is based on having such, and the general public expects this as a minimum from college graduates.

Some students, especially those from severely sheltered homes, have not yet learned how to live with others. College offers this opportunity, especially to those who live in housing on the campus. Some young women know how to get along very well with young men, but they are at a loss as to how to get along with other young women and vice versa. A lot of the idiosyncrasies of both young men and young women are rubbed off in campus living.

In the process of living and let live a number of close friendships are formed on college campuses. Some of these last over a lifetime. Many of them do not only afford congenial companionship, they offer social and business or professional assistance.

Some people apparently never get out of the general category of being a college sophomore. These people are annoying. But somewhat akin to that but not annoying is the person who likes to belong to something that is generally thought to be of value and he or she becomes a loyal alumnus/a of the college. This is good when they will go back to the campus for reunions, go to athletic contests, support the college, etc.

There is some social prestige that comes from having a college degree. Invitations and memberships often come to people with that kind of an education.

A person gets satisfaction from winning. A student has won the initial round when he gets a bachelor's degree. He feels proud of himself and rightly so. He has earned it.

Possibly more than anything else for the individual college student, getting a college degree gives him additional self-respect.

And with all of this, what does society expect of him? To be a leader. That is his opportunity, and the major objective of higher education.

In the background there are parents, brothers, sisters, other relatives, and in some cases wives and children cheering the college student on.

Then backstage (not on the campus except for a few representatives who are usually on stage when the diplomas are distributed) are others who helped pay the bill. These are the community, state, nation, church, alumnae, foundations, and other donors who considered it important enough for the general well-being of everybody to give money to help finance the opportunity for students to get degrees from institutions of higher learning. These people were not only interested in everything mentioned above, they also were interested in seeing students get master's degrees and doctorates. Because the more knowledge we get, the better it is if we use is wisely. They know that we live longer when our universities turn out nurses and medical doctors. They know that we live better when our universities turn out lawyers to help settle our differences. They know that we need better economists to help solve financial problems. They know we need better experts in government to solve our governmental problems. They know we need divinity schools to help us live better lives. Etc.

The quintessence of it all is the advancement of knowledge. More of it has been done in universities than anywhere else. Any student who enters college has the opportunity to go all the way if he has the brains and determination to do it. To make a breakthrough in pure science has applications to follow. They help to solve our problems and give us a better way of life.

As has been seen in this volume, higher education is more than awarding degrees. Higher education offers the opportunity for everyone of college age or level to take either credit or non-credit courses not only on the campus but almost anywhere, and more and more people are availing themselves of this opportunity as evidenced, for example, by the large number of people, enrolled in continuing education courses. This is very important and of great worth in a participatory democracy. Such a government is only as strong as the people who elect the officials who run it. The elected officials will try to follow the wishes of those who elected them. Better demands come from voters who are knowledgeable, thinking people. These demands call for honest, and efficient government that really cares for the people and the nation. These demands call for progress that will improve the quality of living for all citizens. These demands call for planning to meet changing conditions of the future.

Higher education needs more quality controls. Many of the quality controls should have higher standards. There should be better coordination of the quality controls. There should be better enforcement of the standards, nevertheless, higher education has been and is the key factor in making the USA a great nation.

CONCLUSIONS

1. Higher education has not given the people of this participatory democracy enough information about how higher education works. The description of the essentials of higher education in this volume is a step toward filling this need. It should result in better understanding, more participation in, and more support for higher education.

2. A very large number of quality controls from outside and inside of higher education have been identified throughout this description of the essentials of higher education.

3. Throughout the description many other quality controls or incentives or actions have been suggested to improve the quality of higher education. These are not necessarily the only answers, but they can lead to dialogue and then followed by action.

4. College and university administrators have their hands full in trying to assure quality performance in the work of all who are responsible to them. Their supervision does not satisfy some influential groups and remedies must be found.

5. There should be more quality controls in operation within the institutions, such as, every department within the institution should have written standards of operation.

6. There should be better coordination of the quality controls, incentives, and standards in higher education. For instance, a Quality Control Coordinator was suggested in this volume and this person should be located in the president's office.

7. There should be stricter enforcement of quality controls in higher education.

8. No control should tell the teacher what to teach or how to teach it or the researcher what to do and how to do it. However, suggestions from industry and other sources regarding teaching, research and public service should be received and evaluated and then those that appear to improve the quality of the undertaking should be put into operation.

9. Exit Scores testing effectiveness of teaching and Performance Scores testing relevance of what has been taught, as proposed in this volume, should go far toward satisfying those who are calling for measurable indicators of quality in higher education.

10. Now with additional advanced computers on campuses, higher education should give the people all of the information about

their institutions that they desire.

11. Higher education has taught students the art of living and the way of making a living. It has produced the leaders of this nation. It has prepared a more knowledgeable electorate. It has advanced knowledge through research. Other achievements could be listed, but without a doubt higher education has been the key factor in making this country a great nation.

12. Most of the people in this country still have faith in the value of higher education, and now higher education should do more to help them document it.

SELECTED BIBLIOGRAPHY

Outside Controls

Allison, G. T. Essence of Decision. Boston: Little, Brown, 1971.

Anderson, Scarvia B. & Ball, Samuel. The Profession and Practice of Program Evaluation. San Francisco: Jossey-Bass, 1978.

Bennis, W. The Learning Ivory Tower. San Francisco: Jossey-Bass, 1973.

Selden, W. K., Accreditation: A Struggle Over Standards in Higher Education. New York: Harper and Row, 1960.

Board of Control

Burns, Gerald P. Trustees in Higher Education: Their Functions and Coordination. New York: Independent College Funds of America, 1966.

Heilbron, Louis H. The College and University Trustee. San Francisco: Jossey-Bass, 1973.

Rauh, Morton A. The Trusteeship of Colleges and Universities. New York: McGraw-Hill, 1969.

Wicke, Myron F. Handbook for Trustees. Nashville: Division of Higher Education, Board of Education, Methodist Church, 1962.

President

Baldridge, J. Victor; Curtis, David V.; Ecker, George; and Riley, Gary L. Policy Making and Effective Leadership. San Francisco: Jossey-Bass, 1978.

Cohen, Michael D. Leadership and Ambiguity: The American College President. New York: McGraw-Hill, 1974.

Dobbs, Harold Willis. The Academic President: Educator or Caretaker? New York: McGraw-Hill, 1962.

Thwing, Charles Franklin. The College President. New York: Macmillan, 1926.

Organization

Baldridge, J. Victor. Power and Conflict in the University: Research in the Sociology of Complex Organizations. New York:

Wiley, 1971.

Gross, Edward. Changes in University Organization. New York: McGraw-Hill, 1973.

Heilein, Albert C., ed. Decision Models in Academic Administration. Kent: Kent State University Press, 1974.

Perkins, James Alfred. The University as an Organization. New York: McGraw-Hill, 1973.

Money, Accounting, and Budget

Bowen, Howard Rothmann. The Finance of Higher Education. Berkeley, Calif.: Carnegie Commission on Higher Education, 1968.

Cheek, Logan M. Zero-Based Budgeting Comes of Age. New York: American Management Association, 1977.

Green, John Lafayette. Budgeting in Higher Education. Athens, Georgia: University Bookstore, 1971.

Meeth, Louis Richard. Quality Education for Less Money. San Francisco: Jossey-Bass, 1974.

Fund Raising

Curti, Merle Eugene. Philanthropy in the Shaping of American Higher Education. New Brunswick, NJ: Rutgers University Press, 1965.

Hawthorne, Edward L. Fund-Raising for the Small College. New York: Bureau of Publications, Teachers College, Columbia University, 1950.

Pollard, John Albert. Fund-Raising for Higher Education. New York: Harper, 1958.

Seymour, Harold J. Design for Fund Raising. New York: McGraw-Hill, 1966.

Planning

Gambino, Anthony Joseph. Planning and Control in Higher Education. New York: National Association of Accountants, 1979.

Hogarth, Charles Pinckney. Policy Making in Colleges Related to the Methodist Church. Nashville: George Peabody College for Teachers, 1949.

Kieft, Raymond; Armijo, Frank; and Buckley, Neil. A Handbook for Institutional Academic and Program Planning: From Idea to Implementation. Boulder, Colo.: National Center for Higher Education Management Systems, 1978.

Odiorne, George S. Management Decisions by Objectives. Englewood Cliffs, NJ: Prentis-Hall, 1969.

Selection and Performance of Personnel

Elam, Stanley and Morkow, Michael H. eds. Employment Relations in Higher Education. Bloomington, Ind.: Phi Delta Kappa, 1969.

Klopf, Gordon John. College Student Personnel Work in the Years Ahead. Washington, D. C.: American Personnel and Guidance Association, 1966.

Scott, Robert A. Lords, Squires and Yeomon: Collegiate Middle-Managers and Their Organizations. Washington, D. C.: American Association for Higher Education, 1978.

Tice, Terrence N. Resources on Campus Governance and Employment Relations 1967-1977. Washington, D. C.: Academic Collective Bargaining Information Service, 1978.

Faculty

Dykes, Archie R. Faculty Participation in Academic Decision Making. Washington, D. C.: American Council on Education, 1968.

Garbarino, Joseph W. and Russieker, Bill. Faculty Bargaining: Change and Conflict. New York: McGraw-Hill, 1975.

Genova, William J.; Madoff, Marjorie K.; Chin, Robert; and Thomas, George B. Mutual Benefit Evaluation of Faculty and Administrators in Higher Education. Cambridge, Mass.: Ballinger, 1976.

Goff, Jerry A. Toward Faculty Renewal: Advances in Faculty Instructional and Organizational Development. San Francisco: Jossey-Bass, 1970.

Students

Dietze, Gottfried. Youth, University and Democracy. Baltimore: John Hopkins Press, 1970.

Heist, Paul. The Creative College Student: An Unmet Challenge. San Francisco: Jossey-Bass, 1968.

Kavanaugh, Robert. The Grim Generation. New York: Trident Press, 1970.

McGrath, Earl J. Should Students Share the Power? Philadelphia: Temple University Press, 1970.

Admissions and Financial Aid

Astin, Alexander W. Predicting Academic Performance in College. New York: Free Press, 1971.

Doermann, Humphrey. Crosscurrents in College Admissions. New York: Teachers College Press, 1970.

Olson, Keith W. The G.I. Bill, The Veterans, and The Colleges. Lexington: University Press of Kentucky, 1974.

Wechsler, Harold S. The Qualified Student: A History of Selective Admission in America. New York: Wiley, 1977.

Curricula

Dressel, Paul. College and University Curriculum. Berkeley, Calif.: McCutchen, 1968.

Levine, Arthur. Handbook on Undergraduate Curriculum. San Francisco: Jossey-Bass, 1978.

Mayhew, Lewis B. Reform in Graduate and Professional Education. San Francisco: Jossey-Bass, 1974.

Scanlon, John Joseph. How to Plan a College Program for Older People. New York: Academy for Educational Development, 1978.

Teaching

Brown, James Wilson. College Teaching: A Systematic Approach. New York: McGraw-Hill, 1971.

Cross, Kathryn Patricia. Accent on Learning. San Francisco: Jossey-Bass, 1976.

McKeachie, Wilbert James. Teaching Tips: A Guidebook for the Beginning Teacher. Lexington, Mass.: Heath, 1978.

Milton, Ohmer. On College Teaching. San Francisco: Jossey-Bass, 1978.

Research

Boalt, Gunnar. Universities and Research. New York: Wiley Interscience Division, 1970.

Kidd, Charles Vincent. American Universities and Federal Research. Cambridge, Mass.: Belknap Press, 1959.

Palmer, Archie MacInnes. University Research and Patent Policies, Practices and Procedures. Washington, D. C.: National Academy of Sciences, National Research Council, 1962.

Price, Daniel O. University Research Administration Policies. Atlanta: Southern Regional Education Board, 1962.

Public Service

Carey, James G. Forms and Forces in University Adult Education. Chicago: Center for the Study of Liberal Education for Adults, 1961.

Liveright, Alexander Albert. Adult Education in Colleges and Universities. Chicago: Center for the study of Liberal Education for Adults, 1960.

Meyer, Peter. Awarding College Credit for Non-College Learning. San Francisco: Jossey-Bass, 1975.

Shannon, Theodore J. University Extension. New York: Center for Applied Research in Education, 1965.

Library

Doughtery, Richard M. Improving Access to Library Resources. Metuchen, N. J.: Scarecrow Press, 1974.

Edwards, Ralph M. The Role of the Beginning Librarian in University Libraries. Chicago: American Library Association, 1975.

Rogers, Rutherford D. University Library Administration. New York: H. W. Wilson, 1971.

Shores, Louis. Library-College U.S.A.: Essays on a Prototype for an American Higher Education. Tallahassee, Flordia: South Pass Press, 1970.

Guidance

Brown, William Frank. Student-to-Student Counseling: An Approach to Motivating Academic Achievement. Austin: University of Texas Press, 1972.

Brunson, May Augusta. Guidance: An Integrating Process in Higher Education. New York: Bureau of Publications, Teachers College, Columbia University, 1959.

Packwood, William T. ed. College Student Personnel Services. Springfield, Ill.: Thomas, 1977.

Seigel, Max. The Counseling of College Students: Function, Practice and Technique. New York: Free Press, 1968.

Extracurricula Activities

Arbuckle, Dugald Sinclair. Student Personnel Services in Higher Education. New York: McGraw-Hill, 1953.

Baldridge, J. Victor. Power and Conflict in the University: Research in the Sociology of Complex Organizations. New York: J. Wiley, 1971.

Burns, Gerald P. Administrators in Higher Education: Their Functions and Coordination. New York: Harper, 1962.

Johnson, Eldon Lee. From Riot to Reason. Urbana: University of Illinois Press, 1971.

Intercollegiate Athletics

Bronzon, Robert T. Public Relations, Promotions and Fund-Raising for Athletic and Physical Education Programs. New York: Wiley, 1977.

Corbin, Charles B. The Athletic Snowball. Champaign, Ill.: Human Kinetics Publishers, 1977.

Rooney, John F. The Recruiting Game: Toward a New System of Intercollegiate Sports. Lincoln: University of Nebraska Press, 1980.

Shea, Edward J. Administrative Policies for Intercollegiate Athletics. Springfield, Ill.: Thomas, 1967.

Auxiliary Enterprises

Van Dyke, George E., Editor. College and University Business Administrations. Washington, D. C.: American Council on Education, 1968.

Chickering, A. W. Commuting Versus Resident Students. San Francisco: Jossey-Bass, 1974.

Neilsen, S. C. General Organizational and Administrative Concepts for University Police. Springfield, Ill.: Thomas, 1971.

Miller, Richard I. The Assessment of College Performance. San Francisco: Jossey-Bass, 1979.

Buildings and Grounds

Bareither, Harlan Daniel and Schillinger, Jerry L. University Space Planning. Urbana: University of Illinois Press, 1968.

Dober, Richard P. Campus Planning. New York: Reinhold Pub. Corp., 1964.

Green, John Lafayette and Barber, Allan W. A System of Cost Accounting for Physical Plant Operations in Institutions of Higher Education. Athens: University of Georgia Press, 1968.

Russell, John Dale. Manual for Studies of Space Utilization in Colleges and Universities. Athens, Ohio: American Association of Collegiate Registrars and Admissions Officers, 1957.

Alumni/ae

Calvert, Robert. Career Patterns of Liberal Arts Graduates. Cranston, RI: Carroll Press, 1969.

Pace, Charles Robert. Measuring Outcomes of College: Fifty Years of Findings and Recommendations for the Future. San Francisco: Jossey-Bass, 1979.

Pierson, George Wilson. The Education of American Leaders: Comparative Contributions of U.S. Colleges and Universities. New York: Praeger, 1969.

Tauban, Paul. Higher Education and Earnings: College as an Investment and a Screening Device. New York: McGraw-Hill, 1974.

Public Relations

Blumenthal, L. Roy. The Practice of Public Relations. New York: The MacMillan Co., 1972.

Fine, Benjamin. College Publicity in the United States. New York: Teachers College, Columbia University, 1941.

Persons, Christopher Edgar. Public Relations for Colleges and Universities. Stanford University, Calif.: Stanford Press, 1946.

Reck, Waldo Emerson. College Publicity Manual. New York: Harper, 1948.

Standards

McHenry, Dean Euguen. Academic Departments: Problems, Variations and Alternatives. San Francisco: Jossye-Bass, 1977.

Moos, Rudolf H. Evaluating Educational Environments. San Francisco: Jossey-Bass, 1979.

Selden, William K. Accreditation: A Struggle Over Standards in Higher Education. New York: Harper, 1960.

Williams, Robert Lewis. The Administration of Academic Affairs in Higher Education. Ann Arbor: University of Michigan Press, 1965.

Worth

Bird, Caroline. The Case Against College. New York: D. McKay Co., 1975.

Chamberlin, Charles Dean. Did They Succeed in College? New York: Harper, 1942.

Juster, Francis Thomas. Education Income and Human Behavior. New York: McGraw-Hill, 1974.

Miller, Richard I. The Assessment of College Performance. San Francisco: Jossey-Bass, 1979.

ABOUT THE AUTHOR

Dr. Charles Pinckney Hogarth has had extensive experience in higher education. He has worked in both private and public institutions. His work has been in junior colleges, senior colleges, and universities in six states. He has held positions as teacher, registrar, dean, director of public relations, assistant to the president, vice-president, and president. He served as president of a junior college for two years and president of a university for twenty-five years.

Dr. Hogarth received his degrees from Clemson, Yale, and Vanderbilt Universities.

Dr. Hogarth is listed in Who's Who in America, Who's Who in the World, and the International Who's Who of Intellectuals.